GUERNSEY

The second largest Channel Island has escaped the near-metropolitan development of its bigger neighbour, Jersey, remaining remarkably as it was seventy years and more ago. It has great architectural as well as scenic beauty, and its long history and many other attractions for the visitor make it the perfect holiday place for island enthusiasts. This new volume in the Islands series gives a full account of its many-sided aspects.

THE ISLANDS SERIES

*Published in United States by Stackpole
All other titles published in United States by David & Charles Inc
The series is distributed in Australia by Wren Publishing Pty Ltd, Melbourne

GUERNSEY

G. W. S. ROBINSON

DAVID & CHARLES

NEWTON ABBOT   LONDON   NORTH POMFRET (VT)   VANCOUVER

ISBN 0 7153 7341 2
Library of Congress Catalog Card Number:
76–58788

Set in 11 on 13pt Linotype Baskerville and printed in
Great Britain by Latimer Trend & Company Ltd Plymouth
for David & Charles (Publishers) Limited
Brunel House   Newton Abbot   Devon

Published in the United States of America
by David & Charles Inc
North Pomfret   Vermont 05053   USA

Published in Canada
by Douglas David & Charles Limited
1875 Welch Street   North Vancouver   BC

CONTENTS

Photographs: all are by Carel Toms of St Martin's, Guernsey, unless marked to the contrary

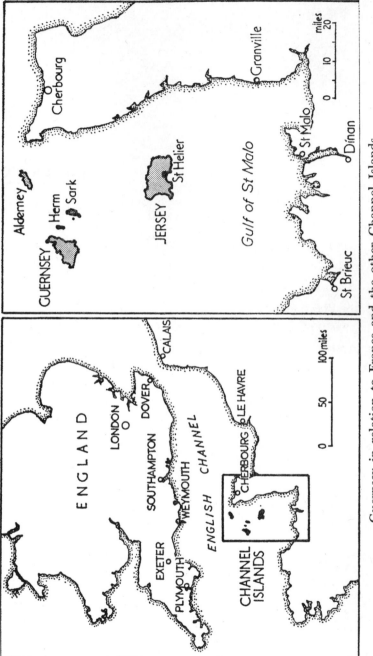

Guernsey in relation to France and the other Channel Islands

1 ITS PLACE IN THE WORLD

OF all the many bays along the shores of the English
Channel, none is more deeply indented or wider
at the mouth than the Gulf of St Malo in north-
western France. From Cap de la Hague at its northernmost
point, the Gulf stretches some 80 miles (130km) across to Les
Héaux and 80 miles south to Mont St Michel. It has been
feared by mariners throughout the ages, for it lies full open
to the swells and storms of the Atlantic and liable to fog and
mist in calmer weather as well. The Gulf generates some of
the most awesome tides anywhere in the world. At St Malo
the rise and fall at spring tide is 45ft (15m), while the currents
off Cap de la Hague regularly run at over 5 knots.

Within the Gulf lie numerous islands, rocks and reefs.
Those on the Breton side are few and small, though the
Roches Douvres, rising unannounced 12 miles from the
nearest land, present a terrible hazard to shipping. The
Norman archipelago, which includes the Channel Islands, is
larger and more complex. In the extreme south the Chausey
and Minquiers groups scarcely rise above the high tides.
Jersey stands virtually alone, though extended monstrously
by wide rocky flats at low water. Alderney forms the landward
end of a ridge that also carries Burhou, Ortac and the fear-
some Casquets. The last group—comprising Guernsey, Herm,
Jethou and Sark—is the most central in the archipelago, the

7

farthest from the Continent (about 40 miles, 65km) and the possessor of the best natural shelter for shipping. The anchorage and harbour of St Peter Port are approached by the Little Russel Channel, which lies, about 3 miles wide, between Guernsey's eastern coast and the small islands of Herm and Jethou. Sark, though not far off in mileage, lies beyond the Grand Russel, a less sheltered and less frequented body of water, and seems at all times to have led a life quite distinct from that of the other islands.

OUTLINE OF THE ISLAND

Guernsey forms roughly a right-angled triangle. The right angle is at Jerbourg Point in the south-eastern corner. The south coast, rocky and picturesque, runs about 6 miles due west from Jerbourg to Pleinmont. Behind this coast lie the 'high parishes', some 300ft (90m) above sea level; in their midst is the island's airport. The east coast measures another 6 miles to Fontenelle; it is rather less simple in outline than the south coast, and bounds in its northern half the 'low parishes', which comprise a rough plain raised little above sea level and occupying the northern third of the island. The town of St Peter Port lies just south of halfway along this coast, at a point where some small valleys descend from the high parishes; here the offshore gradient is steep enough to avoid the excessive shallows found farther north but not, like the south coast, too steep to allow room for safe anchorage. The only other harbour is St Sampson's. It occupies what was once the eastern end of the Braye du Valle, a narrow salt-water channel which runs from St Sampson's church to the Grand' Havre, and at one time divided from the mainland of Guernsey an island measuring about 2 miles by $1\frac{1}{2}$ miles known as the Clos du Valle. The Braye was reclaimed during the Napoleonic wars, and the Clos now forms simply the northernmost section of Guernsey.

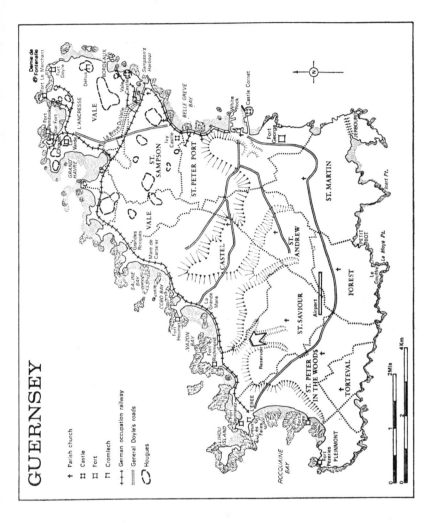

GUERNSEY

The hypotenuse of the Guernsey triangle faces north-west, though it is always known as the 'west coast'. It is 7 miles long from Pleinmont to Chouet, with another 2 miles running east to Fontenelle. Rocquaine Bay, Vazon Bay, Cobo Bay, Saline Bay, Grand' Havre and L'Ancresse Bay succeed each other from south to north along this coast. There is sand in the bays, but most of the shore is fringed with a breastwork of stone extending well out to sea, all the more dangerous and destructive because this western coast directly faces the ocean and lies most nearly in the path of shipping crossing the mouth of the Gulf of St Malo on a course up Channel from Ushant.

GUERNSEY IN THE PAST

The peculiar political status of the Channel Islands has been the key to their history at many times over the centuries; but their geographical position and environment have rarely failed to play their part as well. At different epochs in their past it has been important that they are close to the coast of France, that they lie between the mouth of the Seine and the Bay of Biscay, that they lie between Southampton and Gascony, that they are the southernmost and sunniest parts of the British Isles; no less that Guernsey is smaller and further from France than Jersey, that it possesses a better natural anchorage but not such a sunny exposure, that it lies further from the main Channel shipping routes than Alderney, and a host of other considerations of the same kind.

There is no evidence that Guernsey was inhabited before the New Stone Age, which is not surprising for an island separated from the Continent by sea so wide and deep. But from that time on there is no doubt occupation has been continuous. Neolithic structures, both graves and standing stones, are numerous, and were more numerous, but they cannot be said to differ in kind from those in neighbouring provinces—Brittany comes instantly to mind in this context.

10

In fact for most of its early days Guernsey formed a rather obscure and unimportant appendage to the continental shores of the Gulf.

Small Roman objects are turned up from time to time; but no traces of building are known. Nor is Guernsey mentioned in history before the Antonine Itinerary. This named a list of islands in the outer seas; the earliest modern antiquaries confidently identified each of those listed, and assigned to Guernsey the name Sarnia. Few, if any, modern scholars agree with the identification, but it has stuck now. Sarnia it is for better or worse, from mailboats to sports clubs and from lilies and ferns to flourishing cities in Ontario.

Guernsey with the other Channel Islands formed part of the Duchy of Normandy. In 1204, when the rest of the duchy reverted to France, the islands remained appendages to the English crown, henceforth sharing the ups and downs of England's history and in almost every period meriting a footnote to its more dramatic events.

St Peter Port became an important stronghold and a worthwhile objective of the French in time of war. Castle Cornet was a key fortress in the English defences. Although Guernsey was rarely attacked, it was captured by the French in 1338 and held for seven years.

In 1483 the islands were declared neutral by papal bull, and peace reigned for the next 200 years. At the Reformation, Guernsey adopted the Calvinist faith, which it retained until the Restoration.

In the Civil Wars, with typical contrariness, Jersey sided with the royalists, Guernsey with the parliament. Despite this fact, Castle Cornet was held for the king in the face of superior forces for almost nine years. The Napoleonic era brought real danger of invasion. A large garrison was quartered on the island and a new stronghold, Fort George, was constructed not far south of the old Castle Cornet. With the end of the war in 1815 the garrison forces were with-

11

drawn and Guernsey's importance as an outpost of England's defences was over.

THE ISLAND'S ECONOMY

The livelihood of the islanders was long based on the products of the soil and the sea. Corn was the principal aim of the cultivation of the land and provided the staple food of the people. Fishing too was important and already a source of exports. In the fourteenth century the tax on dried fish accounted for almost a quarter of the Guernsey revenue. The carrying of merchandise between England and Gascony, and later along the Channel coast, brought an increase in trade to St Peter Port and wealth to those engaged in it. The long famous family of Le Marchant, for instance, came from Bordeaux and established themselves in Guernsey by purchasing land with the profits from their merchanting. The Guernsey fisheries were hit hard by the Reformation, which curtailed the Catholic market for fish, and by the discovery of the Newfoundland Banks with their more rewarding fishing grounds. A much-needed new base to the island's economy took the form of woollen goods, the Channel Islanders becoming highly specialised in knitting stockings for export.

In 1689, when the status of neutrality the islands had enjoyed for 200 years came to an end, there began a period when fortunes were acquired from privateering, the wine entrepôt business and smuggling. All three activities were interlocked. Stocks of spirits kept in Guernsey for legitimate purposes were at times diverted to less innocent ends. Ships built as fast privateers came in handy beating the preventive men; and the proceeds of prize sales no doubt provided much of the capital for the entrepôt trade. The long series of wars, mostly against France, in the late seventeenth and eighteenth centuries set the stage for much profitable privateering and smuggling, which reached a peak in the French Revolutionary and Napoleonic wars.

The end of the wars was a terrible moment of truth for Guernsey. The island had ridden high on the boom compounded of wine, spirits and guns. Within a decade all was in ruins. In 1805 the laws for the suppression of smuggling were extended to the Channel Islands. At almost the same time the introduction of the bonding system in Britain deprived Guernsey of its legitimate function as entrepôt for dutiable wines and spirits. Finally in 1815 the end of the war saw the withdrawal of the garrison and the end of abnormal profit from seaborne trade.

There followed a very difficult period during which many expedients were given a trial; the most successful enterprises proved to be shipbuilding and stone quarrying. While the export of stone continued throughout the nineteenth century, shipbuilding went into decline, killed by the introduction of the iron hull. In the second half of the century it was to the land that both Jersey and Guernsey had first to look for salvation. Not for the first time in their history the islanders showed their resilience in adapting themselves to changing conditions in order to earn their livelihood and survive.

AGRICULTURE

Throughout the eighteenth and nineteenth centuries Guernsey and Jersey exported cattle—almost exclusively cows and heifers until the 1870s. At first a dual-purpose beef and dairy animal was produced, combining the Dutch and Shorthorn qualities; later, better results were achieved by specialising in a dairy breed in which Dutch milk quantity combined with Channel Island cream quality. The import of French cattle to Guernsey was prohibited by law from 1819, mainly to prevent French exporters from passing their stock through the island into England free of duty. All imports of

13

cattle, except for immediate slaughter, were prohibited from 1862, though they probably ceased well before. The thorough-bred Guernsey dairy cow was being judged and refined as early as 1835; the Herd Book was opened in 1882, and the dairy herd became a reservoir for the export of breeding stock from about that time on.

Root crops had already assumed a new importance in agriculture. Parsnips were fed to the cattle; potatoes were exported or distilled for spirit. These features were common to both Jersey and Guernsey; but after about 1870 the ways parted. While Jersey continued to export new potatoes, later adding tomatoes grown on the same fields as a second crop, Guernsey turned more and more to glasshouse production. Grapes were exported in respectable quantities as early as 1830 and other fruits followed. The last three decades of the nineteenth century saw the establishment of a flourishing horticultural industry. Tomatoes seem to have first been grown as a main crop in 1884 and by the end of the century were almost the only considerable glasshouse crop.

POPULATION AND VISITORS

The improved speed and regularity of communication with England, resulting from the introduction of steam navigation and railways, not only helped the export of perishable crops but were basic to the other two branches of the island economy which originated in the nineteenth century and grew to maturity in the twentieth—the English visitor and the English resident, neither of whom would have been attracted without regular contact between Guernsey and England.

The flood of visitors has swollen from the trickle of a hundred years ago to some 200,000 a year nowadays, occupying at the peak of the season practically all the 15,000 beds provided for their use. At that time there must be nearly one visitor for

14

every two Guernsey people in the island—and the island is far from being uncrowded at the best of times.

A population of over 53,500 on 24 square miles means a density of over 2,500 to the square mile, or about 3.5 to every acre (as compared with 1.1 to the acre in the Isle of Wight), and the rate of increase of over 14 per cent in the decade 1961–71 was nearly the highest ever.

Guernsey has taken drastic steps to curb the inflow of permanent residents. Houses in the island can normally be occupied only by island families or by those declared essential to the island's economy. The only exceptions are for rich immigrants who may be expected, by the taxes they pay, to compensate for the inconvenience they occasion. They may acquire a house on the special development at Fort George or any houses with a rateable value of over £85: of these there are about 2,000, of which about half are available for occupation by outsiders.

INCOME AND TAXATION

Guernsey's national income in 1975 was in the order of £112 million—a figure which suggests an average income per head quite close to that in the United Kingdom at the same time. A very large proportion was accounted for by imports; the domestic product itself was generated approximately as follows: horticulture 25 per cent, agriculture 1 per cent, construction 8 per cent, hotels and catering 8 per cent, banking and finance 7 per cent, trade and commerce 6 per cent, retailing and wholesaling 16 per cent, manufacturing 5 per cent, public services 14 per cent and private services 7 per cent. Guernsey's specialities among these are seen to be horticulture, hotels and catering, and banking and finance. The vast disparity between horticulture and agriculture, growing and farming, is immediately obvious. Growing, however, may not occupy such a secure place in the economy as it seems to do. Its product has increased little over the last ten years, especially on the tomato side, in spite of valiant efforts in technical modernisation. Its share of island employment is still diminishing, and those in the business are becoming on average older and older, as recruitment is poor. Nor do these figures by themselves prove a threefold superiority of horticulture over tourism, for whereas almost all the product of growing is included in the 25 per cent attributed to horticulture, the benefits of tourism spread well beyond the hotel and catering business. It has been estimated that tourism earns the equivalent of £19 million a year of exports for the island, while exports of tomatoes are worth about £15.5 million and of flowers £5.75 million more. Growing only needs to stand still for a few years more to lose its pre-eminent place.

Investment income is a natural by-product of the well-off immigrant. It has been growing since the war; a recent guess is that it amounts to well over £6 million. The growth of money handling in the Channel Islands is even more recent. Before the 1960s the banks confined themselves to the normal transactions of a small but active community. Now there is a growing number of merchant banks and finance houses with branches or subsidiaries established in both Jersey and Guernsey. The effect has been to add the islands to the 'off-shore finance' world, in which they occupy in some ways a privileged position, for they enjoy unusually stable government for such places and are easily accessible from the financial centres of Europe, especially London. The rentier class on the islands provides some of their business, and those proposing to move in on retirement often start shifting their assets in advance. There are also British people working abroad who consign their sterling savings to the islands to avoid paying British tax, as well as United Kingdom residents domiciled abroad and UK companies with business abroad who may find the islands convenient. There is even a growing

Page 17 The harbour of St Peter Port was completely remodelled by the Victorians, Castle Cornet being united to the mainland by the Castle Emplacement

Page 18 (above) Wrought iron work is a marked feature of the Regency terraces in St Peter Port. The centre building, an hotel, is one of the hundreds of buildings scheduled as ancient monuments; (below left) Office of the Constables of St Peter Port, originally the town house of the Le Merchant family; (below right) pillar box of 1853, claimed to be the oldest in the British Isles

competition with the established Swiss bank business in 'escape' money from unstable countries.

All this money passing through Guernsey is taxed there, albeit at a low rate, and adds usefully to its revenues at very little expense. It is widely believed in England that there is no income tax in Guernsey and that alcohol and tobacco are free of duty there. In fact, of a total States income of £19 million in 1975, nearly 60 per cent was raised by an income tax of 20 per cent and 17 per cent by the impôt, or excise, arising (apart from petrol and oil) almost entirely from alcohol and tobacco. Profits from philately, a mainstay of really dwarf economies, bring the States of Guernsey the negligible sum of £200,000.

THE ECONOMIC OUTLOOK

Guernsey's prosperity in the last hundred years, whether from horticulture, tourism or finance, has relied on the twin foundations of the 'British connection' and the 'special relationship'. Britain's entry into the European Economic Community threatened to undermine the economic usefulness of both, for the Treaty of Rome contains provisions for free trade within the Community, for free movement for employment within the Community, and for homogeneous taxation systems for all members. Very fortunately for Guernsey, Britain managed to gain exemption for her offshore islands from the last two requirements. Guernsey can continue to manage her own finances in her own way and does not have to introduce Value Added Tax, and can also continue to control entry of outsiders.

Horticulture is bound to suffer, however, from the first provision—Community free trade. The industry is ailing already in age-structure of both plant and personnel; the market for tomatoes has ceased to expand, and the Dutch have put up formidable competition on the British market.

The removal of the British tariff will see prices received for tomatoes fall by an estimated 12 per cent; an authoritative calculation is that, if costs went up by the same amount, half the Guernsey tomato growers would be out of business. Things will probably not come to that pass because the same kind of logic would see a fair proportion of the Dutch go out of business too.

Tourism is not threatened so much by the Treaty of Rome as by a secular drift from nearer to more distant destinations, from bracing or mild to hot and sunny climates, from 'home' to 'abroad'. A supple resort can adjust to provide a niche for a special kind of holiday, and Guernsey may in fact be able to do that.

The offshore financial business seems to fit in well with EEC membership. If Guernsey is looking for a prop to the economy in the new circumstances, this might be it. Such business might serve well if it grew in volume; but it is a fragile thing at best, dependent entirely on the toleration of others, some of whom are liable no doubt to fits of jealousy. It may be that Guernsey will use this precarious resource—as it did the equally precarious privateering and smuggling of the eighteenth century—as a means of raising funds with which to improve the general standard of the island's infrastructure and to accumulate wealth to invest in some, as yet unknown, stabler forms of enterprise.

2   THE NATURAL SCENE

FROM the boat which brings the trippers back from a
day's outing to Sark or Herm the Guernseyman can
fully appreciate the form and shape of his own island.
As he looks into the low rays of the setting sun, he sees quite
a simple outline. On the left—to the south, that is—the
island rises abruptly, almost vertically, it seems—straight
from the sea to a height of over 300ft (90m). About 3 miles
along to the right this land lies level at nearly the same
height, then falls away quite suddenly and definitely to a low
plain scarcely above sea-level, so low in fact as to be obscured
by the houses from the boat's view, except for a couple of
detached hills rising on either side of St Sampson's harbour.

Bonamy saw the same in 1749: 'The island is about eight
miles in length and between four and five in breadth. It is
high land in the south and low in the north.' That is the
essential. At more leisure the detail can be filled in: the cliffs
are rarely vertical for more than 150ft (45m) from the
shore, the land then sloping away into a hogbacked form; the
plateau tilts very gently northward over most of its extent;
its surface is interrupted by narrow valleys running north-
westward across it; it ends on the west coast in a series of
embayed bluffs which echo but stand back from the familiar
bay beaches of summer days; the low plain is dotted with
more detached hills than could be seen at first; it seems to be
extended to seaward by the shoals and rocks off its coasts; it is

prolonged round the west coast beneath the bluffs both above and below the tides as far as the Hanois; and finally the plateau and plain meet in a shallow bluff extending east and west right across the island from Cobo Bay to Belle Greve Bay, crowned at its central—though unfortunately its least impressive—point by the church of St Mary of the Castel.

These features are not peculiar to Guernsey. The high plateaux form the dominant masses of Jersey, Sark, Alderney and Herm, and top the coastal cliffs on the coast of Normandy as well. The low plain is particularly well developed in Guernsey; but it can also be discerned in the north of Herm, in the east of Alderney and at Cap de la Hague, as well as in the Minquier and Chausey groups. And the embayed lowlands of Guernsey's west coast can be paralleled at St Ouen's Bay in Jersey, in the north of Alderney, and at many points on the coast of Cotentin.

ROCKS

It might be supposed that these high and low lands would correspond with differences in the geology of the underlying rocks. Geologists do, in fact, distinguish two rock complexes in Guernsey—a northern and a southern, both dating from a period over 570 million years ago; but the boundary between them departs widely from the bluff between plateau and plain and obviously cannot be held directly responsible for it.

The southern rock complex is of metamorphic origin. The principal constituent is gneiss and other rocks account for only an insignificant part of the complex, though their importance in elucidating the history of the whole is sometimes out of proportion to their extent, and they can be studied to advantage at many points where they are exposed on the coast. The gneisses do not make good building stone, being full of cracks; but in the south of the island they were used very widely for field walls and even for cottages when

22

transport was laborious and expensive. The rocks of the northern complex are igneous—having solidified from liquid 'Magma' at great depth below ground under immense heat and pressure. Five phases are recognised with different mineral compositions, ranging from gabbro to diorite, grano-diorite and adamellite. They are all termed 'granites' by the quarrymen whose fortunes they made. The hornblende gabbro of the 'St Peter Port gabbro' is immensely strong and dense, and formed the backbone of Guernsey's stone export business. For road metalling purposes the gabbro when crushed was unrivalled; but for everyday building the Bordeaux diorites, which cover the greater part of the northern zone, are better suited. They are also crushed, but easier to work than the gabbros and strong enough for construction purposes. They can be seen all over the island in houses built between the early nineteenth century when the improvement of the roads made them available everywhere, and the coming of the concrete block, which superseded them for building purposes. One cannot leave the igneous complex without mentioning the Cobo granite—an adamellite to geologists—whose delightful rosy colour glows warmly in the setting sun at Cobo and Saline Bays.

LANDFORMS

The Guernsey plateau and the Guernsey plain cut right across all these geological formations quite indifferently. We can only conclude that they owe their formation to forces at work since the era when the rocks were formed. The best guess we can make at present is that the plateau must have been broadly fashioned by erosion during the Pliocene Age, and possibly levelled by the sea before being raised to its present height during the later part of the subsequent early Pleistocene Age. Opinions differ about the northward slope of the Guernsey plateau, a feature which has been noticed for many years, especially as it contrasts strongly with the more fortunate southward-facing Jersey. The simplest explanation is a tilt during uplift—quite a common phenomenon; but it is more than possible that this is not so much a simple slope as a set of wave-planed platforms cut in the plateau as it rose from the sea. These events of the early Pleistocene Age date from over 2·5 million years ago, antedating the whole of the great Ice Age.

It is the Ice Age which is responsible for very many of the features of the present Guernsey landscape. During the Ice Age, the ice came and went several times over Northern Europe and maybe Asia. During the cold periods which brought the ice there were times, called Inter-stadials, when the ice retreated somewhat though the climate remained severe; there were also periods of warmer climatic conditions—Inter-glacials, during the latest of which we are no doubt now living. The ice itself never reached the Channel Islands, but the scenes the islands witnessed were still dramatic enough. First, it is probable that icebergs calved from sea-ice in the Bristol Channel travelled from time to time to the southern shores of the English Channel and there left their trace, as they melted, in the form of flints and quartzites which are found on the western beaches of Guernsey to this day. Then, each time the icefields grew, vast volumes of water were converted into ice and the level of the oceans fell correspondingly. During the inter-glacial and inter-stadial periods the water was released and the oceans rose, at times higher than they lie at present. In the glacial and inter-stadial times winters were intensely cold and the ground was frozen to some depth. On spring days the sun thawed out the ground's surface and the oozy mess tended to creep downhill, smothering the angles of cliffs and bluffs under a mass of unconsolidated slush, the more stable present-day remains of which have long been known as 'head'. At the same time the severely cold conditions left much ground poorly covered with plant growth, and the strong winds blowing off the ice-caps picked

24

up and carried away the smaller particles as dust, dropping them farther from the ice where winds slackened and vegetation thickened. They form now deposits of fine even-grained yellowish brick-earth, sometimes without structure as dropped by the wind, sometimes inter-bedded with head, and sometimes layered as subsequently re-arranged by running water. This 'loess' or 'limon' covers wide areas in Central Europe and Northern France.

We see in Guernsey the results of most of these processes. The total variation in sea-level over the Ice Age was in the order of 450ft (135m). The seas of the Hoxnian, Ilfordian and Ipswichian Inter-glacials and Inter-stadials all left behind them fossilised beaches where the wave-worn pebbles and rocks which made up the beaches of those times have been cemented together and preserved, often under a blanket of head, to be revealed later either by an advance of the sea or by quarrying and similar activities. The higher of these beaches are found at 90–100ft (27–30m) and 50–60ft (15–18m) above the present sea-level; but the most numerous and impressive, which date from the Ipswichian, are at only 25ft (7½m)—and, given the tidal range in these waters (the rise and fall at spring tide is 29ft), their base is practically continuous with the top of the present beach. There are examples of these fossil beaches—known as 'raised beaches'— on all the coasts, though they are few and small on the southern shores. The finest are at L'Erée, opposite Lihou Island, and at Chouet, in the quarry below the German tower. There are also signs of high sea-level far inland, and the evidence suggests that the whole northern plain, excepting the occasional hills or 'hougues', was levelled by the sea during this period.

Each time the cold advanced over northern Europe the tundra conditions formed head on every slope and cliff, and it is mainly to this that Guernsey owes the softness of its landscape curves. In particular the bluffs between the plateau and the plains to the north and west were much smoothed off; and the present sea cliffs from Pleinmont round to St Peter Port quite possibly trace their sloping and now turfed upper sections to this process, while the steep rocky sections below have since been freed of head by the restless waves. At the same time the bitter winds brought the limon to cover both plateau and plain with a blanket often several feet thick and fertile too. The plateau is the better served in this respect; the thickest cover is about 15ft (4½m) in the east, though this thins out westward and practically disappears above Pleinmont.

At the maximum advance of the ice about 16,000 years ago the sea fell to about 200ft (60m) below its present level and Guernsey, along with the other Channel Islands, must at that time have been reunited with the coast of Europe. As the sea rose, Guernsey, Sark and Alderney, over 10,000 years ago, again became islands, followed by Jersey probably less than 8,000 years ago. The incidents of the return of the sea have left their mark, especially on the island's west coast. Here the sea must have built up shingle or sand spits well to seaward of the present coastline. As the sea-level rose the area between the spits and the bay-bluffs filled with water and became a chain of lagoons, where peat was formed from the aquatic vegetation of the still waters and from the forests which had previously occupied the land. At the same time the spits were forced landwards, sometimes in the process revealing on their seaward sides peats and fossil forests formed in the freshwater lagoons that previously lay in their lee. The puny remains of the choked lagoons can be seen at La Grande Mare and the Mare de Carteret, but place names and records reveal the existence of several more within historical times.

CLIMATE

As its western side lies open to the Atlantic Ocean and as

westerly winds are the commonest in these latitudes, Guernsey is a place of wind and storm, especially in winter. But the Atlantic air has its moderating effects as well; summers are rarely very hot, with an August average of 60° F (15° C), indeed they can sometimes turn out downright wretched— one year the thermometer never topped 65° the whole summer long. Winters are markedly mild; of the last fifty, nine escaped frost altogether, and half saw no more than 3° of it. Snow is recorded surprisingly often, but it is hard to distinguish from sleet, and very rarely lies. The rule of the westerlies is commonly broken for a while some time during the spring, when iron-cold north-easterlies come in—straight from Siberia it seems. The Atlantic air is damp as well as mild of course. The average rainfall is 36in (91cm) and rain falls year in year out one day out of two. The wettest district seems to be around Fort George; in the middle and north of the island rainfall is a tenth less, and even a fifth less at L'Erée in the extreme west.

Sunshine is vital for both tomatoes and visitors. Guernsey averages 1,874 hours a year—as against 1,840 at Sandown (the best in England)—but Jersey totals, at 1,882, were always higher until Guernsey realised it was innocently measuring sunshine at the airport, the least sunny spot in the whole island. A meteorological station was established in 1967 at L'Ancresse in the low country on the extreme northern coast. In the first seven years of operation this station recorded an average of 1,992 hours of sunshine a year compared with 1,896 at the airport and 1,891 in Jersey.

FLORA AND FAUNA

There are at least four reasons why we should expect the flora and fauna of the Channel Islands to differ from those of England. First, the islands lie off the coast of France and can naturally expect to have flora and fauna more French than English. Second the islands lie further south than England, though too much should not be made of this fact, for Guernsey lies only $\frac{1}{2}°$ south of Lizard Head, and Alderney only 10′ south of St Agnes in Scilly. Thirdly, the shores of the Atlantic are almost as mild in winter as the shores of the Mediterranean, and as there is no wedge of cold along the ocean shores between these two mild areas, species can spread fairly easily from one to the other. Last, it is normal for the fauna and flora of islands to differ from those of neighbouring lands, both because some species never reach some islands, and because those that do tend, over time, to grow more or less distinct from their cousins on the mainland. It is the fauna which are, by and large, most affected by the last consideration. Unwinged animals, especially small ones, cannot easily cross the water once it bars their path, while plants can propagate themselves by seed or spore broadcast and carried by chance over water as well as land. As an up-to-date, readable and concise account of fauna and flora, Nigel Jee's *Guernsey's Natural History* is indispensable and it has been widely consulted for the following paragraphs especially where the flora is concerned.

Depending on their size, the islands have a wealth of flowering plants and ferns—richer on average than areas of comparable dimensions in Britain or France: Guernsey has about 900 recorded species compared with Jersey's 1,000, Alderney's 700, Sark's 600 and Herm's 500.

Among the plants found in Guernsey and the neighbouring parts of France, though never or very rarely in Britain, are the wild asparagus, autumn squill and loose-flowered orchid, while *Viola nana* is only known in the British Isles in the Scillies, and rupture wort and the clover *Trifolium occidentale* at the Lizard. Perhaps the most striking species are those which have crept round the mild Atlantic margins of Europe from the Mediterranean, sometimes struggling on to Britain's far western shores as well. Nigel Jee mentions the sand crocus (also at Dawlish, Devon), the small adder's tongue (Scillies), Marquand's sage, yellow bird's foot (Tresco) and yellow vetch. There is also a polyploid form of herb robert, *Geranium rubescens*, which is known elsewhere only in Madeira. *Romulea rosea* var *australis*, a native of South Africa, called 'onion grass' in Australia and found on St Helena and Tristan da Cunha, has recently appeared in Guernsey. Hare's-tail grass has probably been introduced direct from the Mediterranean and the wild gladiolus, *Gladiolus byzantinus*, has escaped from cultivation, its vivid imperial purple flowers glowing in the long grass of some Guernsey meadows as it does amid the green spring corn on its native Sicilian hillside terraces. The minute Jersey fern is found in one location in Guernsey, also two hybrid ferns: *Asplenium x sarniense*, discovered very recently, and *A. x microdon*, re-observed after a long lapse.

Reptiles are few in the islands. The slow worm is found everywhere except in Sark; the green lizard in Jersey and Guernsey; the wall-lizard and grass-snake in Jersey only. The English frog is found everywhere, as is the long-legged continental nimble frog, though it is absent from the adjacent coasts. But the palmated newt and the toad, the *crapaud*, are native only in Jersey, though both have spread to Guernsey within the period of systematic observation.

Among small mammals the weasel is absent from all the islands and the red squirrel from all but Jersey; the stoat is found in Jersey and Guernsey, the mole in Jersey and Alderney, the brown rat in Jersey, Guernsey and Alderney —Sark harbours a specially large race of black rats which have so far kept the brown rat out. As if these permutations were not bewildering enough, the mice, voles and shrews show several subtle and complicated variations. Field mice are present over the whole archipelago, of a variety inter-mediate in size between the yellow-necked mouse and the wood mouse, though closer to the latter and resembling the variety found in the Hebrides. There is a special variety of bank-vole in Jersey intermediate between those of Great Britain and Raasay, but it is not found in Guernsey. Guernsey has, however, a short-tailed vole not found today in Jersey, though it is thought to be identified in the Palaeolithic site at La Cotte; it is of the continental group of short-tailed voles, larger than usual but smaller than the Orkney variety. Lastly there are two varieties of white-toothed shrew in the islands; the continental variety is found in Guernsey, Alderney and Herm, while a smaller one is found, confusingly, in Jersey and Sark.

Insects include the Glanville fritillary butterfly, which is found in Britain only in the Isle of Wight, and the blue-winged grasshopper (also in the Scillies). The topshell *Gribbula pennanti* is unique to the Channel Islands and the adjacent Brittany coast, while some mealybugs are found only in Guernsey.

The island's most famous Mediterranean 'immigrant' is undoubtedly the ormer, an edible mollusc whose range extends out into the Atlantic as far as the Azores and along the ocean's eastern shore from the Gulf of Guinea to the Channel Islands.

3   LANDSCAPE WITH LANDMARKS

WHILE the most vivid impression of the Guernsey countryside must be made on every visitor by the strange world of glasshouses, that unique and insistent ingredient of every view, there is much besides to capture the enquiring eye, much of it more permanent. The glasshouses themselves are set in a matrix of tiny walled fields or 'courtis', punctuated by modest, solid, pantiled farmhouses, the whole permeated by a network of narrow winding lanes and narrow but purposeful main roads, lined as often as not with rows of neat though uninspiring bungalows. From time to time the scene is varied by a church, a chapel, a country house or a hotel, while exploration may lead to a hamlet, a dolmen or a quarry. To understand this fascinating patchwork of landscape it will be necessary to go back to times when very little of it existed in the shape we see now, though the thread of continuous development still links the earliest days of settlement to the present scene.

MONUMENTS OF STONE

The first inhabitants, who, so far as we now know, arrived during the New Stone Age about 5,000 years ago, were capable of crossing the sea and supported themselves by agriculture. They could make pottery without the use of a wheel, cut and polish stone, grow corn and grind it in stone querns into flour. These Neolithic folk have left two principal legacies to the island: the basis of an agricultural and social landscape, and their funerary and religious monuments.

Their dolmens and menhirs, passage graves and standing stones are features of Neolithic culture found all round the Atlantic coasts of Europe, linking these early Guernseymen with Spain and Portugal, Brittany, Wales, Ireland and the far north of Scotland. No one knows for sure what was the purpose of the standing stones. Their positioning suggests that they may have marked such sacred spots as springs or boundaries, or they may have played the part of sacred guardians of the shores and the cultivated land.

Most of these standing stones are simply long rocks set on end with perhaps an underground foundation of small flat stones. But there are two in Guernsey which are much more exciting; these are the carved stones at St Martin's and the Castel. The one at St Martin's, which is called La Grand' Mère de la Chimquière, stands right in the churchyard gateway; she is about 5ft 6in tall (1½m), rectangular in outline as far as the shoulders, but with moulded bare breasts and a suggestion of folded hands beneath. Her impassive face is strongly fashioned and seems to observe the passing scene with emotions that have long passed the stage of approval or disapproval. The carved menhir of the Castel was discovered under the church floor in 1878 and set up in the churchyard. The modelling of this stone is more elementary but perhaps more elemental than that of the Grand'Mère. The breasts are small and no face now appears; but the general shape of the stone is freer and less rectangular, and gives an impression even more suggestive of life and force.

There are excellent passage graves in Guernsey, though not nearly as many as there must once have been, and none on the scale of the magnificent Hougue Bie of Jersey. There is no true 'dolmen' in the island, for a dolmen, strictly speaking, consists of a 'polygon or circular chamber roofed by a single capstone' (Kendrick) all originally buried in a great earthen mound. The Guernsey graves are all 'approached from the east by a narrow passage, and roofed by a series of capstones, placed directly across the uprights, that decrease in size from west to east'. Three of these graves survive—at La Varde, Le Déhus and Le Creux ès Faïes. The third is perhaps the most charged with magic, being untrammelled by locks and fences, and set near the sacred isle of Lihou. In island lore the magic of standing stones and stone burial chambers was a long time dying. The two known sculptured stones are both safe in churchyards; the Trépied, high on Catioroc hill overlooking Perelle Bay and Lihou, was for long the meeting place of witches. Many of the stones marked resting places for the coffin on its traditional journey along the *route de l'église* to the churchyard; others formed prominent landmarks on the route of the Chevauchée de St Michel.

These stones are all that remain in the landscape of the first inhabitants; but it has been suggested by A. H. Ewen (following Susan Harris) that from their time should be dated the continuous occupation of the island's soil, perhaps even the origins of the main civil divisions and settlement sites. The argument goes that there is evidence that originally the land of Guernsey was farmed on an 'open-field' system, implying the cultivation in common of the best patches of soil and the utilisation of the surrounding areas as auxiliary 'waste'—that is, for pasture or fuel. The evidence shows also that the areas of open field, or 'camps', as identified by place names, are distributed very nearly one to each of the present parishes, and are often so placed that standing stones appear near their boundaries but not on the fields themselves. At the same time it is noticeable that recorded commons and wastelands tend very definitely to occur along the boundaries between the parishes. In the six southern parishes it is even reasonable to see the parish churches as centrally located in the probable areas of open field, and at St Martin's there is actual evidence of this arrangement. In the extreme north, in St Sampson's and the Vale, it seems probable that a later, perhaps Celtic, fishing or seafaring folk occupied the coastal areas and established settlements close to the sea away from the older Neolithic centres.

PARISH CHURCHES

Corresponding to the Christian phase of this oldest order of island life are the ten parish churches. They are sturdy—at best attractive, if on the whole undistinguished—buildings, all but one grown into their present shape by accretion, during the course of the Middle Ages, of successive additions to simple stone cells, which no doubt at first replaced even earlier wooden structures.

Their most noticeable features are their towers and spires, which fall easily into three families: St Sampson's, with its unique and archaic saddleback; the Vale, the Castel, St Martin's and the Forest, with rather similar dumpy Roman-cemented spires flanked by spirelets on the tower corners, which give them a distinct flavour of France and strike a strange note to an English visitor; and St Andrew's, St Saviour's and St Peter's, with firm, full, square towers, which sit well in their churchyards and give the impression more of an English parish church, perhaps a solid slow-grown Devon one. The odd man out is the church of Torteval. The medieval building was allowed to decay in the eighteenth century and was pulled down in 1818. The new church was characterised by a most unusual tower and spire entirely unlike anything else in the island; it is quite remarkably round and smooth, tall in proportion, not at all attractive and still uneasy in its setting, though none the less memorable.

34

Page 35 The Guille-Allès Library and French Halles seen from the balcony of the New Markets. The library was built as Assembly Rooms in 1780

THE RURAL SCENE

The churches and parishes and a few place names survive as reminders of the old order, but the open fields have disappeared and the countryside has for long been one of intimate lanes and tiny walled enclosures. Peter Heylin wrote of Jersey and Guernsey in 1661: 'Both islands consist very much of small Inclosure, every man in each of them, having somewhat to live on of his own . . . in Guernsey the walls are for the most part made of stones, about the height and fashion of a parapet.' And so it is today. This fundamental transformation of the landscape did not take place in a day. It resulted essentially from a change in the economy—from a subsistence to a money economy—hastened by the requirement to remit feudal dues to overlords, both temporal and spiritual, who lived outside the island, and by the investment in the land of money earned by the island's seaborne trade. The usual procedure was to turn to crops not liable to tithe: apples for cider or roots (commonly parsnips) for stock. Both called for enclosure, especially to prevent the straying of animals over the land in winter, which was an integral part of the old system. This practice of 'banon', which long held up agricultural progress, was finally suppressed in 1717. Between the fourteenth and seventeenth centuries the leading island families managed, by persistent application of sharp practice, condoned by the ruling island institutions which they monopolised, to possess themselves of the greater part of the ecclesiastical lands and common wastes belonging to the Crown and the village communities, so that today the sandy desert of L'Ancresse is the only extensive common land remaining in Guernsey.

An essential element of the new system was the farmhouse, the nerve centre of the enterprise. Though none survives from the Middle Ages, those of the sixteenth, seventeenth, eighteenth and even the nineteenth centuries are among the most delightful elements of the Guernsey countryside, and do much to redeem it from the strictures levelled at it by Skinner in 1827: '. . . a number of small inclosures, intersecting each other, all formed of stones piled without cement, affords no very pleasing or picturesque object to the traveller'.

The medieval farmhouse must have been very simple, probably wooden and thatched, with a large hall, open roofed and open fired, serving all living purposes, and an ancillary store or buttery at one end. Remains of a possible ancestor of such a house were found not long ago at Le Feugré, Cobo. They have been identified as a 'long house' of the tenth century, and thus the oldest habitation known in the Channel Islands. There were low stone walls on the outside—perhaps originally surmounted by wattle and clay work or directly by sweeping eaves—and posts supporting a roof over the space within, where there was also a fireplace.

The earliest farmhouses extant are more advanced structures; they have chimneys and glazed windows, and a wooden screen across the end of the hall, which has become the kitchen and common living room, while the buttery has become a parlour. There is also some kind of upper floor for bedrooms and storage, which is approached by a ladder or by a staircase enclosed in an exterior round tower—this attractive and characteristic feature of the older Guernsey farmhouse is not often seen from the road because the tower always projects from the back of the house. The oldest houses of this kind date from the sixteenth century, but they continued to be built for another 150 years.

They were mostly constructed of rough stone from some neighbouring quarry, secured with a limeless rather feeble clay mortar, and roofed with thatch and lit by transom windows. Many doors are framed by the characteristic Guernsey arch, consisting of two shoulderless arches, one outside the other, of big stones set flush with the wall of the

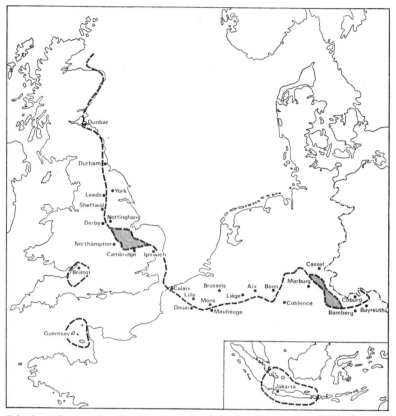

Limits of pantiles in Europe (and Indonesia); the shaded areas
are intermediate in character

house, giving a massive but flattish effect—quite distinct
from the single, shouldered arch typical of Jersey. By the
middle of the eighteenth century most farmhouses were
built with two storeys throughout, often of dressed stone and
with sash windows arranged either on a symmetrical 'nine
window' plan or with a small parlour allowing only seven
windows on the frontage. The thatch had been replaced by
tiles or slates. Where the house had originally been thatched,

39

the stones which projected from the chimney stacks to protect the vulnerable upper edge of the thatching were left high and dry some feet above the lighter and thinner tiled roof. Later generations, not understanding what had happened, dubbed them 'witches' seats'.

The tiles used in all the Channel Islands were invariably pantiles, the delightful double-curved tiles which originated in the Low Countries and spread all over northern Europe, coming into England in the seventeenth century. Their remarkable North Sea and Baltic distribution is shown on page 39, but there are three outliers further afield, one in the core of the Dutch Indies, another round the port of Bristol and the last in the Channel Islands. No satisfactory explanation has ever been given for this curious departure in the Channel Islands from the practice of both the neighbouring French mainland and of those parts of England with which the islands were in closest touch at the time.

GLASSHOUSES AND BUNGALOWS

Since the middle of the last century the Guernsey countryside has seen another widespread revolution. There are now few districts, and still fewer roadsides, where the typical landscape of courti and farmhouse dominates the scene. Nowadays it is the glasshouse which is found everywhere, especially in the northern parishes; and with the glasshouses goes the classic grower's house, a small but comfortable two-storey dwelling, rendered, with a slate roof and perhaps some ornate Victorian ironwork embellishment. The proportions are rarely happy for a rural setting, but exaggerated 'style-building' is rare, and all is in apple-pie order, including the intensively cultivated front garden, a 'riot of colour' the summer through.

Even where glasshouses are rarer, the visitor who does not leave the main roads will quickly conclude that the whole island has become one continuous suburb. And while a short détour down a lane in the upper part of the island will usually soon dispel this impression, it remains a valid reaction on the main roads, which over the last hundred years have suffered from an advanced attack of ribbon development. These strings of bungalows, villas, and miscellaneous detached dwellings are accepted by now as a part of the island scene. Long continuance has even endeared them to the islanders, and they have been commented on favourably by visitors for their spick and span neatness and cleanliness, their bright gardens, and their generally small scale, which fits them into the small-scale landscape better than might be expected and perhaps better than they individually deserve.

CASTLES AND FORTS

Guernsey today is a military backwater, but this is quite a recent state of affairs. For much of its history, Guernsey was an important place of arms, and as far back as history goes was continually in peril from the seaward side.

The face of the island is scarred—or embellished, according to the point of view—with relics of military works which range from simple earthen banks and round towers to elaborate machiolated structures and intercommunicating concrete complexes. The changing scale and form of these works has depended partly on the changing state of the art of war and partly on the changing value that the world's calculations have assigned to Guernsey's strategic position.

The earliest fortifications probably date from a time when the island was of marginal strategic significance, and the main preoccupation of the inhabitants was to save their skins and meagre possessions in the event of chance descents by raiders or pirates. This must surely have been the purpose of the works at Jerbourg. Though there are persistent references during the Middle Ages to a 'Castle of Jerbourg', all that can be seen today—and perhaps almost all that there has ever been to see—is a series of three banks and ditches which obviously ran from cliff to cliff, cutting off a peninsula about half a mile long and a quarter broad to form a ready-made place of refuge for the population in the troubled times after the breakdown of the Roman Empire.

To find the earliest solid 'castle' in Guernsey we must move down from this airy detached promontory to a very different scene, a dank lowland, now a puddly backwater of meadowland, earlier a formidable marshy tract. In this deserted and forgotten corner, only some 400yd (350m) behind the busy Banques road, lie the once-dilapidated, recently spruced-up, remains of the Château des Marais, for centuries aptly known as 'Ivy Castle'. Here is the genuine breath of the Middle Ages: stone parapets, vestiges of a central keep, a watery moat; no primitive hiding place this, but permanent quarters for clanking men at arms, set close to the heart of the island and prepared to defy capture by intelligent and costly organisation of difficult marshy terrain. The earliest mention of the Château des Marais is in 1244; it is then already referred to as *'la vielle chatellenie'*, which suggests that it dates back before the loss of Normandy in 1204 and is probably a local Norman seigneural fort or baron's castle, perhaps headquarters of the Cotentin fief on the island (as suggested by Miss Edith Carey).

Like Jerbourg, Ivy Castle was an inward-looking, isolated fortress inaccessible from the seaward side. To enable Guernsey to fit into a new, wider strategy covering the whole English Channel and its approaches, a different kind of fortification was called for after 1204—a castle that could be maintained and supported from the sea, by the king of England himself, and preferably one that could command the roadstead at St Peter Port which alone gave Guernsey importance in the military calculations of the time. Such a fortress was Castle Cornet, thought to have been conceived and built in its original form very soon after 1204, on a site which was useless as a refuge for the people of the island and not particularly convenient as an administrative centre, though it long served as such. What it did have was a superb defensive position, surrounded by the sea except at the lowest tides, and immediate command of the all-important anchorage. No doubt the English strategists calculated that the castle could be held by England even if Guernsey fell into enemy hands. It is an irony of history that on both occasions when Castle Cornet held out against a power in Guernsey it was then in the hands of enemies of the English government, on whom the tables were thus unkindly turned. The first occasion was during the Hundred Years' War, when a French force which had captured Guernsey in 1338 held on in the castle for nearly five years after being expelled from the rest of the island apparently with ease. The second was during the Civil War, when the royalist deputy governor, Sir Peter Osborne, shut himself up in the castle with a small garrison and maintained his position there against the parliamentary island for nearly nine years before surrendering the place on honourable terms.

The principal feature of the medieval castle was the great round central tower, or keep; it rose from the highest part of the rock separating two walled baileys, one to the north, the other to the south. Nothing can be seen of it today because it was blown up in 1672 when lightning struck the powder magazine. The tower had long been a white elephant; Le Patourel declares that it was already over-vulnerable to artillery by the end of the fourteenth century. As the power of guns increased, the castle was repeatedly remodelled, the most important occasions being in the late sixteenth and the eighteenth centuries. Sir Thomas Leighton, the island's governor from 1570 to 1609, provided the entire castle with a system of platforms extending out below the medieval enceinte. These were designed to carry batteries and their

43

construction conformed, as far as the site allowed, to the 'ivy leaf' shapes first devised by Leonardo and developed by engineers everywhere for siting batteries in defence of fortresses. In the eighteenth century the whole of the south or inner bailey of the old castle was filled in to make one great gun platform named 'The Citadel'.

By the time the Citadel was built, Castle Cornet was already becoming completely out of date as the principal fortress of Guernsey. Its site was too cramped to house an adequate garrison, and it could be over-shot by the guns of the day from the higher ground inland. It was necessary, if Guernsey was to be secure, to start from scratch on a completely new work, which should be a regular fortification able to hold out against attack by a properly equipped enemy already landed on the island. For this purpose a fort needed to be well sunk in the ground with plenty of thick turf to take the enemy's shot; with deep, well-enfiladed ditches to prevent sapping, and with a free field of fire without dead ground to deter frontal attacks. For such conditions a gently rising plain or plateau formed a site as suitable as rocky hills or promontories. The situation chosen was a virgin one, a plateau surface close to the southern edge of St Peter Port, where in 1780 arose Fort George, which was to remain for the next 160 years the military headquarters of Guernsey.

Fort George has always been a centre of controversy. Its purpose, its effectiveness, its needs, and even the disposal of its site have all caused tempers to rise or heads to wag. In the first place, its purpose was very limited. In 1797 General Lord Dalrymple commented 'If Fort George is not to be considered as the last resort of the Troops; I do not know how to estimate it at all . . . The Fort is completely out of Reach of the Road, out of Sight of the Town and Beach and in short covers nothing but the space of Ground it contains.' The point had not been lost on the people of Guernsey either.

The Royal Court averred in the same year that 'the in-habitants of this island to a man consider Fort George as a great evil' because they could see that it was intended as a refuge for the British garrison in case of invasion while they themselves would be abandoned to 'the mercy of a savage enemy'. It took all the tact and insight of General Doyle, when he became lieutenant-governor, to overcome this attitude; and this was only achieved by an understanding that in case of a retreat the island militia (and their families!) would retire within the lines along with the regular troops 'and share with us our last biscuit'. Even the efficiency of the fort for the limited purpose defined by Lord Dalrymple was called in question. Lord Cornwallis was of the opinion in 1798 that 'Fort George after all would be a very indifferent Fortress'.

The main trouble was the field of fire. Not only were there several knolls and ravines outside the perimeter from which the batteries might be approached in dead ground, but the whole area was also criss-crossed with a dense network of typical Guernsey field banks, 'solid banks of earth four to five feet thick and equally high', which obviously afforded ample cover to an enemy attempting to approach the fort and seriously limited its value as a strongpoint. The removal of these banks was vigorously opposed by the Royal Court (whose consent was required for 'compulsory purchase') ostensibly on the grounds of the illegality of such inter-ference with the rights of individuals, but really because of their general opposition to the whole concept of Fort George as a garrison refuge. Such bitter opposition to British military plans in time of war may sound strange today; but at that time it was obviously nothing unusual. General Doyle wrote in a despatch of 1803: 'Tho' there is no disloyalty, yet there exists even now, such a tenacity of their Privileges, and such a Jealousy of the Military, as requires the greatest prudence to counteract . . . A Battery cannot be Erected without the

Consent of the States, who must have Eight Days Notice; a Gun can scarce be moved without a Law Suit . . .'

Fort George was virtually destroyed by a British air strike the day before the landings in Normandy in 1944. For a long time it lay derelict, as Army land will; but eventually in 1958 the whole issue was sold by the War Office to the States of Guernsey for £25,000. A committee of the States recommended in 1960 that most of the site be sold off for high-class residential development; this sparked off a controversy which roused high feelings at the time. A petition attracted over 10,000 signatures; but the contractors offered over £100,000 and the development has gone ahead.

While Jerbourg Castle, Château des Marais, Castle Cornet and Fort George were each in their day the principal strongpoint of the island, at most times other fortified places were maintained as well. Along the high, cliffed coast between St Peter Port and Pleinmont there are a few breastworks and Martello towers in the bays, some lookouts above; but, from Pleinmont northwards, forts are found on practically every headland: Pézeries, a pretty little star-shaped fort at Pleinmont; Fort Grey, or Rocquaine Castle, a small, prominent cup-in-saucer tower in Rocquaine Bay, now a maritime museum; Saumarez, at L'Erée; lumpy Richmond, looking like a barrack block; Hommet, at Vazon, rich with a central magazine, a ravelin, two bastions, emplacements for Victorian swivel guns, and a great deal of German work as well; Pembroke and Star, at the far north-west; Plomb, or Le Marchant, at the northernmost point; Doyle, with its romantic drawbridge, at the north-east corner, not to mention Martello towers and isolated batteries or lookouts. There is even a round stone tower built in 1855 on the rock of Bréhon in the middle of the Little Russel. Older than any of these is the Vale Castle, which seems to have done the same duty on the detached isle of the Clos du Valle as Jerbourg Castle did on Guernsey proper. It is now an attractive and finely sited medieval shell set on a hill overlooking St Sampson's harbour.

These ancient works are not the only evidence of war that the visitor to Guernsey sees. There still exist—too numerous to mention individually—many signs of the role that the Nazi-occupied island played, or was supposed to play, in World War II. Tons upon thousands of tons of steel and concrete were poured into the German defences of all the Channel Islands. So extreme was the concentration of fortification here that it is assumed only Hitler himself could have been responsible for such absurdity and only he could have had the authority and pigheadedness to persist in it. In 1944 there were eleven heavy batteries with thirty-eight heavy guns on the Channel Islands, while on the 600-mile-long French coast between Dieppe and St Nazaire there were just eleven heavy batteries with thirty-seven heavy guns. The garrison of Jersey and Guernsey at the same time comprised a division, amounting with ancillaries to 35,000 men. And all for nothing! The Allies' landing in France simply passed these strongholds by and left them to surrender lamely at the end of the war. The Germans typically built good and solid; their concrete defences remain as part of the landscape, a mellowing reminder of a page of island history.

4   ST PETER PORT

AIR passengers miss one of the finest experiences Guernsey has to offer, the approach to St Peter Port from the sea. The view that greets the traveller arriving by steamer or yacht is one of the most enchanting in the British Isles. The complicated but shipshape harbour works occupy the foreground, flanked to the left by the romantic bulk of Castle Cornet. Immediately behind lies a wall of varied but time-reconciled buildings seeming to rise several storeys high direct from the harbour side and broken at one point to half-reveal the firm outline of the Town Church topped by its small but dignified and commanding spire. Behind this first rank, the houses appear to climb in tiers on the backs of those in front to culminate in a skyline adorned with towers and ornaments which, though dear to Guernsey people, are perhaps not all worthy of their splendid setting. A strange site for a town—and an awkward one it is now proving to be—but it was logical enough when it was chosen. In the Middle Ages the overriding need was for shelter for the anchorage and landing beaches; and if you want a hillside to protect the anchorage, then an awkward site for the adjoining town is the price you have to pay.

THE TOWN CENTRE

Immediately behind the Old Harbour the hills approach

quite close to the shore, leaving a narrow shelf 10–30ft (3–9m) above the tide which has afforded space for the present High Street and the Pollet. At either end of this shelf, streams have worn valleys into the plateau edge—a small one to the north followed by the Truchot near St Julian's Avenue, another to the south, much deeper, longer and more impressive. Around the mouth of this larger valley is the original core of the town, with the Town Church at the seaward end. St Peter's structural outline as an irregular cruciform building with aisled nave, chancel and transepts, and a handsome tower at the crossing, was complete by the time of the Reformation. In the following centuries its interior was filled with box-pews and galleries and its outside encrusted with shops and

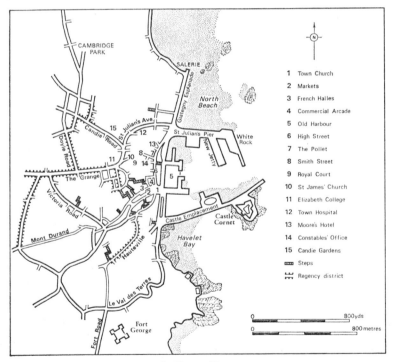

St Peter Port

houses. In addition the whole north aisle except the transept was walled off, the western end doing duty as a vestry and artillery store, while at the eastern end the ecclesiastical court sat in a first-floor room and the space beneath housed the parish fire engines. The Victorians cleaned it up inside and out; the open airy church of today with its sense of space and grace is largely their legacy. So, partly, is the faintly 'continental' feeling, for the new tracery in the windows was copied from originals in Beauvais, Caen and elsewhere in the Flamboyant style which flourished in France but never in England.

Other parts of this old quarter have been transformed since the eighteenth century, being given dignity and charm by several acts of private and public enterprise. First, in 1780, came the Assembly Rooms, a fine concept centring on a spacious first-floor room now occupied by the Guille-Allès Library and approached through an arcaded lower storey. The Assembly Rooms were created by subscription among twenty leading island families who exercised their veto on admission, thus causing considerable ill-feeling for many years among those excluded. The arcade was quite small but the period after 1800 saw the progressive rehousing of all the markets in the large heterogeneous range of market buildings which is still in use today.

Between 1815 and 1831 Guernsey was lucky to have the services of a first-class architect, J. Wilson. His work, which lent distinction to several parts of the town, included the fine frontage with delicate Ionic ironwork on the side of the markets opposite the French Halles, and the bold but rather gloomy façades on either side of Fountain Street. At about the same time Guernsey was brought right up to date by the erection of a pedestrian shopping precinct. This attractive little corner of refuge, known as the Commercial Arcade, is superbly sited between the markets and the High Street. It made, however, no fortune for its creators, the brothers Le

Boutellier, for it had to be hewn at enormous expense out of the granite hillside which rises sheer behind it.

Nowadays, the heart of St Peter Port lies undoubtedly in the High Street. It is at the junction of the High Street, Smith Street and the Pollet that on a Saturday morning the full tide of Guernsey existence is to be observed in safety— blessedly, for this little central area is a traffic-free zone. The district was once favoured by the aristocracy for their town houses: the Brocks' in the High Street has been turned into shops, but the De Saumarez' in the Pollet survives nobly as Moor's Hotel, and the Le Marchants' in Lefebvre Street as the parish constables' office.

In the seventeenth and eighteenth centuries the courts (which in the Middle Ages used to sit in the Town Church) and the meetings of the States all came to be held in a mean little building off the Pollet; it had been the grange of the royal fief and was known as the Plaiderie. This was replaced in 1799 by the dignified but rather dull granite structure at the top of Smith Street which now houses Royal Court, States and Greffe. The interior was naturally decorated in Regency style, and embellished soon after with stairs and domed toplight by the architect Wilson; but when the courtroom was renovated after the German occupation it entered someone's head to decorate it in a fine but somewhat unnecessarily incongruous William and Mary style.

The strong but rather hidden-away Town Hospital gateway of 1742 is another of the town's notable features; and the lanes which climb up and down hill from the main streets are also delightful to explore.

THE SUBURBS

The public buildings of central St Peter Port make altogether an excellent impression for a town of only 15,000 inhabitants. Nonetheless the most attractive and

51

GUERNSEY

striking feature of St Peter Port is probably not the centre
at all but the suburbs. Take the road up St Julian's
Avenue past the College or up Cornet Street from the
Town Church; or better, climb the 145 steps from the
town centre direct up the hillside by Clifton or Constitution
Steps, and you are in another world, a world of Regency and
Early Victorian spaciousness, the suburban quarters on the
plateau top into which the town expanded when it broke
loose, with the profits of smuggling and privateering, from
the narrow limits of earlier times. Before that time, the town
was cramped awkwardly in the narrow site by the seashore.
The expansion onto the plateau top made possible the laying
out of regular terraces and the profusion of distinguished
suburban houses standing in their own gardens—gardens
often romantically exotic with the touch of camellia, myrtle
or palm which comes easily in Guernsey's climate. The heart
of this verdant and elegant world is the Grange, but it
extends also to Cambridge Park and Queen's Road and Les
Gravées, and finds an echo in Hauteville. Terraces and street
houses of the same period and slightly earlier are well seen
in Clifton, Doyle Road, Lisle Terrace and Eaton Place, all
near the Grange; also in Hauteville and Mont Durand, and
even on a humbler level in the Victoria Street quarter.
Guernsey people may be wryly thankful to the German
occupation in one small particular: it saved their fine iron
railings from the panic melting pot which ate up so many
of those on the mainland.

The plateau-top area does not consist entirely of dwelling
houses. It has its public buildings as well, and these are
doubly significant because they stand at the higher level
and consequently dominate the skyline.

Wilson has been at work in this district too. His is St
James' the Less, built in 1817–18 as an English-language
church for the new quarters of the heights. The Doric
pedimented west front looking on the street, with its fine

52

Page 53 (above) The Sealink car ferry leaves St Peter Port. Castle Cornet on the right; (below) Château de Rocquaine, also named Fort Grey, is now a museum. Le Creux ès Faïes is on the right of the distant tower

Page 54 (left) St Martin's, a typical island parish church. Exceptional is La Grand'Mère de la Chimquière, a prehistoric stone figure at the churchyard gate;

(right) typical farmhouse with initials of original owner on the arched granite doorway, dated 1711

and regular proportions and attractive iron-railinged fore-court, can evoke only respect. The delicate Ionic tower above, though it sits a little awkwardly on the pediment, forms the most accomplished element in the skyline. The interior has nothing like the same quality; this may prove fortunate because St James' has been abandoned as a place of worship and can only hope to survive by being put to another use—as a concert hall, possibly—which would mean remodelling the inside of the building.

Just across the street is Elizabeth College, also by Wilson, but nothing like so successful. The College is dressed up in Gothic details, though the masses are in their way as Classical as St James' own—Classical, but bulky, lumpy even, and finished in a kind of schooly-brown Roman cement which does nothing to relieve the effect of drabness. Luckily, to enhance the skyline, it has a spiky if rather dumpy tower—something which Carey Castle, a rectangular shape of the same period and kind, on the northern hilltop, lacks.

The Victorians made their contributions to the skyline too. The visit of Queen Victoria in 1846 was commemorated by the Victoria Tower, an assertive piece of work typical of its period, by a local architect, with sturdy rough stonework and a beetling machiolated crown to it. Not far away is St Joseph's, the principal Roman Catholic church of the island. Though the work of Pugin, it dates from the very end of his life and is unremarkable except for the spire, which is the tallest construction in Guernsey and a worthy silhouette.

THE TOWN'S FUTURE

The limits of the town were certainly long fixed for legal purposes, because in the town the préciput, or right of the firstborn to inherit the farmhouse, was not enforceable; and these boundaries may have marked the defensible perimeter. When in 1683 the States sensibly banned thatched roofs in

D

the town, the Court ordered stones to be set up marking the barrières de la ville as they were then legally defined. These stones, which the parish constables set up in 1700, can still be seen around the streets of St Peter Port today, one near the telephone kiosk by the Town Church, others at the foot of Rosemary Lane, at the top of Tower Hill Steps, in Smith Street and in the Pollet.

St Peter Port has its problems as well as its graces. The decaying quarter is one that is common to most towns. A walk up to the area round Trinity Square will give some evidence and emphasise the special problems that arise from the restricted site of the town.

The restricted site in fact, picturesque though it is, lies at the bottom of most of the town's problems. Room is short for car parking, for circulation, for expansion of the shop and office quarters, and especially for the conference hall, entertainment centre and other developments that are needed to keep Guernsey attractive to visitors who will soon be off to Spain instead if Guernsey cannot offer more on a rainy day than it does at present. A few years ago there was a harebrained scheme for mooring the *Queen Elizabeth* off Glategny Esplanade to fill all these gaps in Guernsey's appeal. Since then a much more realistic scheme has been under examination—and one in keeping with Guernsey's tradition of cautious daring—no less than the reclamation of the whole North Shore, the triangular area between the White Rock, the Salerie and Glategny Esplanade. Already there are proposals for access roads, car parks, conference centres, hotels, gardens, shopping precincts, entertainment centres and so on. It seems a tall order for a surface of some 40 acres; but Guernsey has always been a small place and has become quite accustomed to fitting quarts into pint pots.

5   TRADE AND TRANSPORT

THE best-known panorama in the Channel Islands is the view looking out from St Peter Port over the Little Russel, taking in the town and harbour in the foreground, Castle Cornet to one side, Herm and Jethou immediately opposite, and Sark in the offing. This makes a grand and moving prospect on a summer's evening; but its significance goes much wider and deeper. It is to the possession of this magnificent stretch of water, sheltered from the south-west, with reasonable access to land and protection from a neighbouring strong point, that Guernsey owes much of its place in history and no small part of its individuality.

Peter Heylin saw this very clearly in 1661 when he wrote: 'The principall honour and glory of this Island, I mean Guernzey, is the large capaciousnesse of the harbour, and the flourishing beauty of the castle . . . an harbour able to contain the greatest Navy that ever sailed upon the Ocean; fenced from the fury of the winds by the Isles of Guernzey, Jet-how, Serke and Arme, by which it is almost encompassed. A place not to be neglected in the defence of it, and full of danger to the English State and Trafick, were it to fall into the hands of an enemy.' He was referring, of course, not to the harbour as we see it today, but to the roadstead or anchorage which preceded it. In his day even the 'old harbour' was incomplete; but it is described in its finished state by Bonamy in 1749 much as it is now: 'It is built in the form of an half moon, with the moles or peers extending like two bended arms into the sea. The top of the peers is smooth and paved with Swanidge stone; and there are posts for the ships to fasten their cables. These serve as a walk for the inhabitants, there being walls on each side. This harbour is capable of containing near an hundred vessels great and small.'

THE HARBOURS

The transformation of the harbours of St Peter Port and St Sampson's is almost entirely the achievement of Victorian Guernsey, and could reasonably be regarded as its finest monument. The regularisation of the shoreline at St Peter Port did indeed precede the Queen's accession. The quay to landward of the Old Harbour at St Peter Port was constructed during the years 1775–83, and Glategny Esplanade was built up in the years following the great storm of 1821. The work on the new harbour was on a much more extensive scale and the great expense contemplated led to a corresponding hesitation on the part of those called upon to pay. The idea of the new harbour was first officially mooted in 1830, the States decided to build in 1851, the foundation stone was laid in 1853, and ships landed and embarked passengers at the White Rock landing stage from 1864. Construction had taken a great deal less time than decision.

Since that time the harbour works have not stood still; the lighthouse was added in 1867, the weighbridge in 1891, the London berth in 1899. But the most important addition has been the New Jetty, of 1923, which provides ample berthing space for the mail boats even today. Instead of being built of granite like the rest of the works it was constructed of steel and concrete. These were in those days comparatively daring materials for marine works and not perfectly understood, with the result that the money saved on granite in the 1920s may well fall as a charge for reconstruction in the 1970s. Room was made in the early harbour plans for a floating dock in the area now named the Albert Dock; but they came to nothing and it is doubtful if the island has suffered much in consequence. Even without the floating dock the new harbour of St Peter Port was a stupendous undertaking for the place and time. The enclosed area of water was raised from $4\frac{1}{2}$ acres (2ha) to more than 80 acres (32ha) within a dozen years, and this has sufficed for over a century of unprecedented traffic growth. Only now is talk being heard of further remodelling of this area, and even the plans of today do not envisage changes as fundamental as those effected in the last century. Recent additions which help to keep the harbour up to date are a container berth, graced by cranes far taller than any previously seen there, and a roll-on roll-off facility.

The granite for the harbour works came largely from Les Vardes in the north and from the island of Crévichon, between Herm and Jethou; but vast quantities of filling material were also needed, and these were taken from La Vallette, on the shore of Havelet Bay—giving rise, incidentally, to the fine promenade round by the bathing pools.

St Sampson's, the only other harbour in Guernsey worthy of the name, occupies, close under St Sampson's church, the eastern end of what was the Braye du Valle, the arm of the sea which once separated the island of the Clos du Valle from the mainland of Guernsey. This is also almost entirely a Victorian creation, the works being undertaken in sections between 1839 and 1898 in response to the ever-increasing demands of the stone trade. The harbour was protected by breakwaters from the seaward; rocks were cleared from the fairway; and bays on both north and south sides were filled in, supplying at the same time quays for ships to come alongside, flat land for loading gear and, initially, space for the disposal of ballast from incoming vessels. This last was a

59

perpetual problem at St Sampson's, for sailing ships ready to export stone came in without cargo but loaded with ballast of clay or chalk which had to be offloaded on arrival. Special enclosed dumping areas were created north and south of the harbour entrance; but much was still deposited outside, so that in places the Russel was shallowed from 30 to 22ft (9 to 7m) by this process.

MERCHANTING AND PRIVATEERING

A remarkable feature of the maritime activity of the harbours and roadstead has been its persistence over the centuries in spite of the constantly shifting geographical value of the position of the island. In this drama of the sea the stage of trade and war is set differently in each period; but in almost every act there is a part for Guernsey to play. When King John lost Normandy and his other possessions in northern France, he and his successors right down to 1453 retained possession of Gascony and the wine country of Bordeaux. Ships bound from Gascony for England were forced to run the gauntlet of French territory right round Brittany, and the first friendly port they reached would normally be St Peter Port, which became an important way-station in that trade; the link was so close that more than once the wardenship of the Isles was combined in the same person with the seneschalty of Gascony.

When the Channel Islands were granted a privilege of neutrality by bull of Pope Sixtus IV in 1483, Guernsey was free to participate in the trade of the Gulf of St Malo and in that between Gascony (once more in French possession) and the mouth of the Seine. It took advantage of this situation to develop a flourishing entrepôt trade, which lasted well into the seventeenth century, supplemented by the export of stockings and other island produce. In the middle of the seventeenth century the Guernsey 'fleet' comprised eighteen vessels of between 8 and 120 tons, though none of them was built in the island, and Heylin could report: 'nor do they trafick only in small boats between St Maloes and the islands, as those of Jarsey; but are masters of good stout barks, and venture into all those nearer parts of Christendom'.

In 1689 William and Mary abrogated the Channel Islands' neutrality and the islanders immediately started on a brilliant career of privateering—in fact, a prize court had already been set up as early as 1666, and it is legitimate to suspect that the official abrogation had merely terminated a preliminary period of 'shamateurism'. During the wars of William III and Anne the Guernsey privateers proved themselves the scourge of French inshore commerce. They lay in wait for coasting traffic all round the west coast as far south as the Gironde and Arcachon, as well as operating in their 'home waters' of the Gulf of St Malo. During the War of the Spanish Succession they took some 750 prizes of a total value of about £100,000. Guernsey privateers formed perhaps 15 per cent of the whole British privateering fleet, they were often quite tiny—one of 4 tons is recorded—but a typical Guernsey privateer of the time might be a sloop or galley of 30–50 tons carrying 4–8 guns and a crew of 30–60 men. The capital invested would almost certainly be local, as would be most of the crew, though there might easily be deserters from the fleet on board as well.

Privateering eventually dried up during the Napoleonic wars for want of prizes, but in the course of the eighteenth century other trades had been built up, both legitimate and clandestine. The smuggling business, in which Guernsey served mainly as an entrepôt for English smugglers, was vast and well organised. It brought great wealth to the island, much of which is reflected in the fine houses of the inner suburbs of St Peter Port. 'So great was the traffic,' says one authority, 'that many fortunes were realised simply by the manufacture of casks.' But the effects did not end with the casks. The spirits and tobacco for smuggling had to be brought into Guernsey, and this gave rise to a considerable number of other legitimate businesses. Until 1805 wine imported into the United Kingdom was required to pay duty immediately on passing over the quays, with the result that merchants needed very large capital resources if they were to carry any but quite small stocks of wine. But in Guernsey there was no duty on wine; so the English merchants were able to use Guernsey as a huge bonded store where they collected their stock of wine, matured and stored it, and drew on it as required for their business. For storage there was excavated under St Peter Port a vast warren of magnificent cellars, many of which survive to this day—some being used for everyday storage, while a couple form a romantic and authentic setting for a nightclub and discothèque. These new commercial links did not stop at simple import and export. Some complicated triangular—not to say quadrangular, even hexagonal—trades were developed. For instance, brandies exported to Madeira were exchanged for wines for the West Indies; thence rum was taken on for Quebec; at Quebec provisions for Newfoundland; thence fish for Portugal and the Mediterranean; finally wine for Guernsey again.

Up till 1815 the trade of the island's merchants was carried in ships built elsewhere; but after the end of the Napoleonic wars Guernsey quite suddenly became an important centre of shipbuilding. It looks as if some of the fortunes made in the war may have been put to work in this way when peace came. Guernsey-built sailing ships found their last resting places all over Europe, from the Needles and Owers to Zara and the Gulf of Finland, and farther afield amid the coral of the Torres Strait and the ice off Newfoundland, in Little Curaçao and on Haiphong Bar. Particularly disastrous seem to have been the River Plate and the River Thames, Terceira and Flamborough Head. The *Clio*, a brig of 215 tons, even managed to wreck herself on the White Rock, within sight of

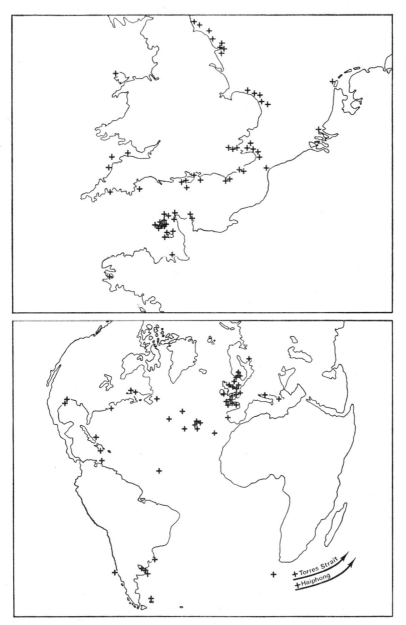

Recorded last resting places of Guernsey-built ships, 1821–1910
(E. W. Sharp, 'The Shipbuilders of Guernsey', *Reports and
Transactions Société Guernesiaise* 18, 1970, 478)

the yard where she was built. The last Guernsey-owned sailing ship seems to have been the schooner *Sidney* of 112 tons, which ended up as a Q-ship in World War I.

Although iron and steam were to bring immense benefits to Guernsey, at first they laid a limiting hand on the commercial relations of the island. Guernsey yards were unsuited to the building of the new ships and Guernsey capital was on too small a scale to finance steamship operations. The spacious days of the wide-ranging Guernsey merchant marine were over; even the special position of the Channel Islands in the navigation of the southern shore of the English Channel was undermined by the greater reliability and freedom of movement which resulted from the use of steam power. All this meant that Guernsey was forced through the nineteenth century to rely less and less upon merchanting and more and more upon exporting once again the produce of her own soil and labour; and providentially this is what steam navigation enabled her to do, by establishing for the first time a fast, reliable and regular link with England.

CHANNEL SERVICES

Regular cross-channel packets were in fact instituted by government some years before steamers came in, and they must have improved communications considerably. The first service began on the outbreak of war in 1778, when a cutter was transferred from the Dover–Calais service. She ran fortnightly till 1783. The service was re-introduced in 1794 on the resumption of war, this time with two cutters, the *Rover* and the *Earl of Chesterfield*, of 80 tons, which maintained a weekly service till 1811, when a third cutter made Wednesday and Saturday sailings possible. There were also traders running to England at this time, but their services were not very convenient. 'A passenger never embarked in these traders,' says Tupper, 'without a bottle or two of wine and a basket of provisions, as the passage frequently extended to two days and nights, and often longer, sometimes to five and six days.'

Steamers

The first steamship to be seen in the island was the *Medina*. Variously recorded as being of 65, 85, 100 and 150 tons, she had been built at Cowes in 1822 for the Isle of Wight run. She was chartered by Col Fitzgerald of the 72nd Regiment to bring his family and possessions from England, and arrived in Guernsey on 10 June 1823. The next day she ran an excursion to Jersey taking 140 passengers, and also the band of the Town Regiment of Militia, which provided entertainment on the passage over and a rendering of the National Anthem on arrival at St Helier; but on the return journey they are recorded as being 'affected by the heat'. The excursion seems to have allowed several hours ashore in Jersey and a heavy swell was encountered off Corbière on the return journey, circumstances which between them may have aggravated the effects of the heat on the band. The unfamiliar sight of the *Medina*'s smokestack almost inevitably set up a false alarm as a 'ship sighted on fire'; but authorities predictably differ as to whether the laugh was on Jersey or Guernsey this time.

Only a year later almost to a day two regular services started between the islands and the mainland. The *Ariadne*, 197 tons, 72hp, built at Rotherhithe by W. Evans, was the candidate of Southampton, whose merchants were backing her. The *Lord Beresford*, 81 tons nett 160 gross, 60 or 70hp, built at Bristol by William Scott, was partly financed in the islands. She ran to Portsmouth in her first year, but in 1825 both ships plied to Southampton, running on alternate weeks at the same rates.

The Post Office, whose packets were now at a considerable disadvantage, took steps to turn their Weymouth service over to steam—the 162-ton *Watersprite,* the first steam packet, arriving in Guernsey on 8 July 1827.

By the 1830s the *Lord Beresford* and the *Ariadne* were both owned by limited companies—respectively the British and French Steam Navigation Company and the South of England Steam Packet Company and these companies and their successors brought new ships on to the Channel Island run, sometimes entering into fierce competition and fare-cutting, but more usually sharing the business amicably.

In 1840 a new era began with the opening of the London & South Western Railway to Southampton. Over the next couple of decades the railways entered the Channel Island business and established a pattern which was to survive till 1961. The London & South Western Railway ran boats to Southampton (to which the mails had been transferred in 1845), and the Great Western Railway ran boats from Weymouth, each in connection with their own railway services. The same services were maintained by the Southern and Western Regions of British Railways until 1961, when the system was simplified by the concentration of all boats on Weymouth. In the early days passenger services ran also, for longer or shorter spells, to Plymouth and Falmouth, Topsham and Exeter, London and Brighton; but all these fell out during the railway era.

Freight

Cargo ships have always run to a much wider variety of ports than the passenger services, though the same trend towards simplification was to be seen at the height of the railway era. After World War II Shoreham and Portsmouth came especially to the fore, though Weymouth continued to hold its own in the freight business as well as in the passenger services.

Four-fifths of the general cargo now comes to Guernsey in containers, on pallets, or on Lancashire flats, and the tomato crop all goes out on pallets. The 'container revolution' has been quickly followed by the 'roll-on roll-off revolution', though for Guernsey there are disadvantages as well as advantages in this. Twice as many vessels could be required as for present methods of shifting cargo; and those visitors who have hitherto managed without their cars, or have hired small ones on the island, may be tempted to bring in larger vehicles, thus adding to the pressure on narrow and crowded roads and demanding boat space at seasons of heavy tomato movement.

Passenger services

Since the days of the *Ariadne* and *Lord Beresford* the passenger ships on the Channel Island service have kept pace with improvements in ship design generally. The first iron ship on the run was the *South Western*, 204 tons, in 1843; the first with screws was the *Griffin* in 1865; the first built of steel the *Laura*, 641 tons, in 1885; the first with turbines the *Caesarea* and *Sarnia*, both 1,505 tons, in 1910. Turbines were rather late in application because they were at first of little use on the overnight services of the time where speed was not crucial. Paddle-steamers lingered on till 1899 because they drew less water, always an important consideration in these parts.

Among the regular steamers, the *Lydia*, *Stella* and *Ibex* of the 1890s were built for 24 knots or more. It was in 1899 that the *Stella* was wrecked with heavy loss of life on the Casquets while proceeding at a racing speed in heavy fog; the railways at last agreed on a pooling of services, thus reducing the competitive pressure of building faster vessels. Since then the average speed has been about 20 knots. Tonnage has increased steadily since the 1820s, rising markedly following the introduction of steel in the 1890s and since World War II. The present-day *Caesarea* and *Sarnia* have a much higher tonnage than their predecessors,

67

though they are only a few feet longer. Hydrofoils run regularly from Guernsey to Jersey and St Malo and, in summer, twice a week to Alderney.

ROAD SERVICES AND RAIL SYSTEMS

No public railway has ever operated in Guernsey but there is a Guernsey Railway Company. Rather confusingly, this company operates motor omnibuses only, but it started life more appropriately by running the Guernsey Tramway.

For the first ten years the trams were operated by the Guernsey Tramway Company Ltd. The track ran from the Picquet House in St Peter Port to St Sampson's Bridge. It was laid down in 1877 and commenced operations in 1879. The early 'trams' comprised an engine with two cars, a saloon car for the first class and an open-sided car for the second class. The first engine was described in the *Star* as 'about 9ft long, 5½ft broad, consumes its own smoke; can be driven at 20mph but regulation speed 8mph; can be pulled up in 5ft; cost £700; Merryweather type similar to those in use in Paris; 10hp, 2 cylinders, 7in diameter, 14in stroke, 9ft 6in overall, 7ft wide; height from rails 9ft; 110lb pressure'.

In spite of fares of 2d in second class and 3d in first which seem reasonable enough today, the number of passengers steadily declined. Competition from horse-drawn buses, which had been running since 1837, was too keen, and the tram was forced out of business in 1889 for eleven months. It was rescued by the Guernsey Railway Company in the same year, and in 1892 was converted to electricity. In 1895 the horse buses were bought out for £4,500; but in 1909 a new threat appeared in the shape of the motor bus. The trams, which for many years were still cheaper to run than buses when fully loaded, were at length forced out of business. The last tram ran on 9 June 1934.

The Guernsey Railway Company had set themselves up as bus operators, competing effectively with the other companies of the day: Guernsey Motors (which had begun operating as far back as 1919); Paragon, of St Sampson's; Blue Bird, of the Vale, and Watson's Greys, of St Martin's. The situation is simpler today. The Greys continue to run the service to Pleinmont via Forest Road; but all other services are operated by the combined GRC and Guernsey Motors, which merged in 1954 and absorbed Paragon and Blue Bird in the early 1960s. Happily the two companies kept their well-known separate routes and green and maroon liveries. Together they hold a stock of about a hundred buses, and even on a winter weekday run over 400 departures from town.

Though the tramway closed in 1934, this was not the end of the story of rails in Guernsey. Only nine years later there was a much more extensive rail system in operation. To carry the vast weight of materials needed for their fortifications, the German army laid about 20 miles of track in 1943. The stretch from St Peter Port to St Sampson's remained until the liberation, though the remainder was removed well before.

The main line, of 90cm gauge, ran from St Peter Port Harbour to St Sampson's, and then continued (with a short-lived spur to Bordeaux beach) to L'Islet, where the railway works were established. From there spurs ran across L'Ancresse Common to points on the north coast, while the main line went on round the bays of the west coast as far as L'Erée. There were feeder lines of 60cm gauge as well. The whole of the main line has since been traced by enthusiasts. It ran along footpaths, drives and roadways, across fields and private gardens, through walls and greenhouses. It necessitated the demolition of remarkably few houses, and there are even recollections of the Germans being persuaded to re-align the track to avoid houses on the route, or in one case a field of potatoes. The track was laid on a 2ft stone bed, or in concrete on public roads. The severest gradient seems to have been one of 1 : 44 between Vazon and Cobo. Not much is known about the rolling stock. Most of the score of locomotives were four-wheelers powered by steam; but there were a few diesel standbys on the main line and more on the 60cm feeders.

AIR TRAFFIC

The first aircraft to be seen in Guernsey were some French military flying-boats which were based on the Castle Emplacement in 1916. They were two-man open FBAs and Telliers and originally communicated with base by carrier pigeon. Their job was to hunt German submarines and they actually sank one.

Flying-boats were used to establish the first commercial service after the war too. There was a service to Southampton by Supermarine Sea-Eagles in the summer of 1923. The crossing took $1\frac{1}{2}$ hours—seventy-three arrivals are recorded in 1924. Another flying-boat service started in 1931, but it did not do much better. An airfield was needed—but where was there room for an airfield in Guernsey of all places? Upper Torteval, Vingtaine de l'Epine, L'Erée, La Villiaze and L'Ancresse were all suggested. A field at L'Erée was used for a time by a service of Westland Wessexes; but for the permanent aerodrome the site eventually chosen was at La Villiaze. One hundred and twenty-six acres were purchased, 130,000cu ft of soil shifted, and 7 miles of Guernsey field banks removed.

The aerodrome was finished in 1939 and for a year operated civil flights before becoming an RAF base for a fortnight and then the landing ground of the German occupation force. When the Germans ceased to benefit from it, it was put to civil use again, and has since gone on from strength to strength. The equipment has been constantly

Page 71 (above) Daffodils are not such an important crop as they were. They are now picked in bud and bunched in tens – Common Market practice; *(below)* the high plateau of the south with characteristic glasshouses, farms and bungalows (*Aerofilms*)

Page 72 (*left*) Tomatoes grown under glass are the island's chief export; (*below*) boxes of them being loaded at St Peter Port harbour for consignment to the UK

brought up to date, runways cut in number from the original four but the survivor lengthened. Even the terminal building has been extended several times, though rarely, it seems, quite catching up with the traffic, which has grown to over 40,000 movements and over 400,000 passengers a year.

6   INDUSTRIES

A S the bases of livelihood have changed through the years, different industries have occupied from time to time important, sometimes dominant, places in the economy, though few have survived for more than a century and most not so long. While dairy farming, horticulture and fishery are flourishing concerns today, this does not mean that the wheel will not turn again. If cultivation of fruit and flowers should suffer the contraction that is forecast by some, Guernsey may turn towards light industry and many see this as at least an ancillary future staple.

KNITTING

The first known industrial episode was knitting, which replaced fishing in Tudor times and reached its apogee under the Stuarts. 'The principall commodity which they use to send abroad,' wrote Heylin in 1611, 'are the works and labours of the poorer sort, as waste-cotes, stockins, and other manufactures made of wooll.' Stockings seem to have been the most successful of these products and Paris their most usual destination, though they were well enough known in England too. So profitable was this occupation that there were even complaints of fields being left uncultivated while men, women and children devoted themselves to their

74

knitting. The products, at first based on wool derived from the flocks of the island, were soon in such demand that wool was regularly imported under a licensing system from England. At this period such specialisations in the products of cottage industry were common all over Europe and could arise quite independently of local raw material so long as idle hands were available.

It is unlikely that the knitted sweater which is now called a 'Guernsey' was ever an important article of manufacture, though there is no reason to suppose that knitted gear for island fishermen and seamen has not been produced domestically for a very long time. Today 'Guernseys' made in a special traditional pattern by island knitters are quite a flourishing business, and they are many an islander's favourite kit for messing about in boats or even for messing about in the garden, while visitors carry them home as practical souvenirs of a Guernsey holiday.

EXPERIMENTAL ENTERPRISES

The period following the Napoleonic wars saw a blossoming of industrial activity, though not many of these ventures had any lasting success. They included tobacco and snuff, Roman cement, ropes and cordage, liqueurs, paper, beer, soap, candles, quinine bark, flour, bricks, tiles, vinegar, cider, and Glauber and Epsom salts. Sugar confectionery flourished mightily for a few years in the 1840s when English confectioners moved to Guernsey with their workforce to take advantage of the lower duty levied in England on manufactured than on raw sugar; but the loophole was soon plugged. Roman cement, flour, bricks and beer no doubt simply served the island market, as may also have been true of the vinegar, soap and candle works. The remainder, with the exception of tobacco and snuff, were short lived, and few survived into the present century. Pipe tobacco is being

75

made in Guernsey still, as were cigarettes until 1965; but strangely enough there is little continuity with earlier manufacture. The firm at work now set up as wine merchants in 1830, and was sold to a Mr Bucktrout in 1866. It dealt thereafter in groceries, wines and tobaccos, retail and wholesale, not taking up the actual manufacture of tobacco goods till 1918 when the grocery side was given up. The number employed used to run to about seventy.

SHIPBUILDING

After the Napoleonic wars, Guernsey quite suddenly became an important centre of ship-building. Most ships were built for the island's merchant traders, who had acquired considerable wealth from their wartime privateering and smuggling. The shipyards were all, excepting a small one at Grand' Havre, on the east coast, at first near the town on the South Beach and at Glategny and Longstore, where the stumps of piles which supported launching ramps can still be seen. Later the main activity was at St Sampson's harbour, where many craft were built for the stone export trade. The construction of the coastal road and esplanade hastened this shift, as launching then had to take place rather awkwardly across the new road, a section of the sea wall being demolished and re-built on each occasion.

Within twenty years sixty-five vessels had been constructed in Guernsey, and nearly 300 were built there altogether, of which 86 were schooners, 79 brigs and 59 cutters. They were of course small, ranging from a cutter of 9 tons to the 656-ton *Golden Spur*, a full-rigged ship built at St Sampson's by Peter Ogier in 1864. She was described in the *Guernsey Press* in 1937: 'Her frame was constructed of French navy oak, her inner and outer planking was of teak and green-heart timber, and all her fastenings were of copper. She had a round stern, upon which was the shield with the Guernsey coat of arms,

76

and her name was in gilt letters, which had been tastefully carved. Her figurehead was that of a life-sized courtier in the dress of the reign of King Charles.' Only one steamer, the *Commerce* of 120 tons, was ever built in Guernsey, in 1874; she came from the same yard as the *Golden Spur*, as did the island's last ship of all—the ketch *Sarnia*, 120 tons, in 1894.

The coming of steam propulsion and iron construction brought shipbuilding to an end in Guernsey, the yards there being unsuited to the new demands. But there is still a ship-yard by St Sampson's harbour with a slip to take vessels of up to 600–700 tons. It carries out the repair of local and British ships, and services the hydrofoils which operate between the islands, though it does no construction work.

STONE QUARRYING

The extraction and export of the island's stone can be traced back deep into the eighteenth century, but the industry was another of those that blossomed in the years following Waterloo. It was encouraged not only by the turn of fortunes in Guernsey at the time but also by the ever-increasing demand in England for road-building material, both setts for paved streets and spalls for macadamised roads. Tests carried out on the Commercial Road showed that Guernsey stone lost only 4–5lb per foot after seventeen months of wear, while Dartmoor granite lost $12\frac{1}{2}$lb and Aberdeen blue $14\frac{3}{4}$lb.

The stone exported was almost all hornblende gabbro and diorite, which occur in the northern part of the island and are too hard to use in everyday construction in Guernsey. Material for local building purposes has been won from numerous small quarries yielding many varieties and qualities of stone all over the island. Most prized of these are the austere monumental granites of L'Ancresse and the much-loved warm rosy granite of Cobo. The gabbro and diorite were exported in steadily increasing quantities throughout the nineteenth century and up to World War I, when over 400,000 tons were being sent away every year. There has been a continual decline from then on, exports in 1972 totalled only 34,000 tons, and declined till today the export of stone has practically ceased altogether.

An island-wide count has revealed 268 disused quarries in Guernsey. Two-thirds of these are in the Northern Parishes, and such is the concentration in some parts that the country looks from the air like a giant colander, pitted with the remains of worked-out exploitations. As most large-scale quarrying operations descend below the water table, a disused quarry normally fills with water and, amidst the bustling life of an active horticultural district, each forms a curious enclave of desolate peace. Approached up an over-grown lane or glimpsed across a stone wall, the still water lies sullenly in its circular cup, walled with perpendicular granite faces rendered mysterious by irregular growths of bramble and ivy.

But not all the quarries are dead—four are still working— and there are plans for expansion and rationalisation. The demand for the traditional cubes, kerbs and spalls has almost entirely fallen off, and labour difficulties restrict the dressing of the island stone for building. The main production is now of aggregate for modern road building and for concrete, though one quarry specialises in rockery stone and crushed stone for site filling, horticultural compost, hoggin, etc. The quarries supply island markets only, and today the industry employs a tiny proportion of the 800 men who worked the stone in 1926.

A Guernsey quarry in full production is a sight—and a sound—not easily forgotten. The depth of the quarry, which at times necessitated the use of a 'tray' suspended on wire cables to raise the stone and sometimes even the quarrymen; the din of the crusher situated right alongside the quarry; the dust and bustle on every side impress themselves irresistibly upon the imagination and form a striking contrast to the purposeful warm green quiet and order of a tomato glass-house.

FARMING

The area of land under cultivation has been contracting steadily over most of the last half a century. In 1920, of the 24 square miles (38,800 vergees*) of Guernsey about 18 square miles (26,625 vergees) were under cultivation. By 1974 it was only 9 square miles (about 14,350 vergees)—a fall from 74 to 37 per cent. Of the land under production about a quarter is devoted to horticulture; almost all the remainder goes to maintain the Guernsey herd, the mother herd of the famous Guernsey cattle found and loved in dairying areas in every corner of the world.

Fifty years ago the export of these cattle was a flourishing business. The cattle farmer was a man of note, commanding high respect, the guardian of an honourable and lucrative tradition. Standards of breeding were high, improvements were constantly striven for. Recognition came from successful sales; from prizes and awards at the shows held under the auspices of the all-powerful Royal Guernsey Agricultural and Horticultural Society (dating from 1817), and by the efforts of the country parishes, which combined to mount the now traditional and variegated North Show, West Show and South Show. Every cow on the island—and there were over 5,000 as recently as the early 1930s—was a pedigree Guernsey, with an entry in the Guernsey Herd Book, and the whole herd was guaranteed against contamination by strict laws regarding the import of cattle.

The Guernsey herd subsists today and it is still as closely

*The vergee is the common measure of land in the Channel Islands. Of course, the Jersey and Guernsey vergees do not agree; it takes about $2\frac{1}{4}$ of the Jersey, but $2\frac{1}{2}$ of the Guernsey, vergees to make an English acre—$2^{23}/_{49}$ to be exact.

protected and cherished. But its place in the world is rather restricted now, with exports more or less a thing of the past. The sole business of the island's cows for some years now has been to provide the island with its daily milk, though at times more has to be imported. The cow population has run down to around 2,600 in milk—a number thought to be about right for their purpose. Although the population of the island is rising slowly, the demand for milk—especially fatty milk of the Guernsey kind—does not rise so fast; also the production of milk per cow is continually being increased by the devotion and cunning of the island's farmers. Yield has risen by over a fifth in the last twenty years, and yield per vergee by over a quarter.

The traditional method of grazing cattle can still be seen quite often on the island. The cows are put out in the fields tethered with a rope about 6yd long; they crop the grass within their range closely and thoroughly, and are then moved on and tethered anew. This is an economical method so far as the grass is concerned and is probably responsible for the docility of the Guernsey cow's disposition; but it is wasteful of labour. That did not matter much when the farmer had only a few cattle and a large family to do the work. But many present-day farmers have neither; so in addition to tethering, they may run their cattle in the small fields or use electric wire to confine them to 'paddocks' or corridors. Some have even gone over to 'zero grazing', and keep their stock in stalls fed on bought-in cattle feed and on maize and silaged hay from their own fields.

The little fields, or 'courtis', with their thick stout earthen baulks topped with furze, are thought to have originated as orchards in the heyday of the cider economy. They have survived the tethering process pretty well intact, but the new methods, particularly 'zero grazing', tend to rely more on hay than growing grass—and more on machinery than on scythe and tether-rope—so that the baulks are beginning to become a nuisance. So down they are coming, and down they will come in still greater numbers as the years go by, and future generations can expect a Guernsey landscape different from the one we have known and can still by and large see today.

Fields are getting bigger, and so are farms. The new methods are based on full-time occupation of personnel, whether of the farmer's family or of paid labour. And this means that a farmer, to break even, must keep at least enough cows to occupy one man, which may well mean forty cows. At present, of about 170 dairy farms, no more than 40 have that many, and only 60 farms in all have over thirty. It looks as if in years to come the number of dairy farmers in the island will fall; but perhaps not as drastically as the economic arguments would suggest, for already many Guernseymen keep Guernsey cows as much for the honour and satisfaction as for the money they bring them.

At present a cow needs about four vergees of land for pasture and feed. So with the small herds that are still typical of Guernsey it is natural that dairy farms should be small as well; in fact the average dairy farm has around 60 vergees (24 acres), and only seventy of the 200 farms have as much land as that. Most dairy farms are neither wholly owned nor wholly rented; a typical farmer has probably inherited a farmhouse with a bit of family land, and has rented extra fields adjacent or in the same part of the parish when opportunity has offered. The result is seldom cohesive and often inconvenient; but it has at least the merit of flexibility, as rented land may be released or taken on as occasion demands or as a farmer's requirements rise and fall. The old method of buying land with 'rentes' of quarters of wheat is now very seldom resorted to.

Island farming has at present a very narrow economic base; Guernsey cows produce Guernsey milk for Guernsey consumption. The agricultural economy may well be broadened

81

in future in two different directions. Jersey is already producing long-life milk for export, and Guernsey might reasonably
follow suit. More drastically, the whole conception of the
monopoly of the Guernsey breed may be challenged. Legislation now permits the importation—under strict control—
of Charolais semen; the first cross-bred cattle are in the field,
and the next few years may see the inauguration of a beef
herd based on this Guernsey–Charolais cross and aimed at
producing meat for export to continental markets.

HORTICULTURE

While farming feels itself restricted on an area of about
11,000 vergees, horticulture—or 'growing' as it is commonly
termed in Guernsey—makes do with 3,500, of which nearly
three-quarters is under glass. The manpower situation, however, is quite different; according to the census of 1975, the
11,000 farming vergees employ about 250 persons, compared
with 650 on the 5,000 horticultural vergees. The contribution
to the island economy is even more markedly disparate—
agriculture contributing an estimated 1 per cent of the
domestic product against horticulture's 25 per cent.

This dominance of horticulture is a phenomenon of the
last hundred years, but its roots go back somewhat earlier—
heated greenhouses in possession of the island's gentry being
recorded in 1792. This was common enough elsewhere at
that time, but by 1830 the development in Guernsey was
described as remarkable: nowhere in Europe were so many
greenhouses to be seen, according to one observer; and there
was even a small export of grapes and pears. This produce
came from the private grounds of the gentry, who must be
allowed to be the founding fathers of the industry, though
by 1840 Duncan could already report glasshouse building
for profit by even 'persons living little above the class of
cottagers'.

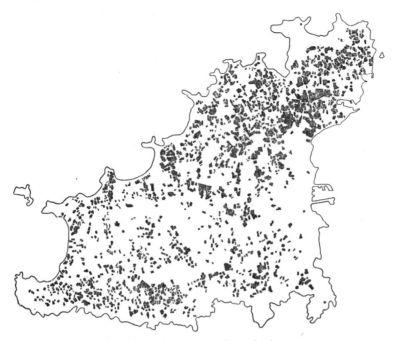

Land under horticultural glass

Such precocious development before the existence of either
steamships or railways must have been based on remarkable
natural advantages over places closer to the markets. The
maritime climate, with its cloudy skies, high winds and
low summer temperatures, might not be expected to be
favourable for fruit and flower cultivation. High winds
are, in fact, an almost unmitigated disadvantage for growers,
who suffer from the cooling effect of the airstream passing
over their glass—and the average annual windspeed in
Guernsey is 20 knots, against 15 in the Isles of Scilly and $12\frac{1}{2}$
in the Solent. But the wind does clear pollutants out of the
air smartly, and this was particularly important in the old
days when coal was the heating agent and even the Welsh

83

anthracite then used darkened the air above the island until at peak times it looked from a distance like a squadron of battleships at full steam ahead. Low summer temperatures are not a serious handicap because they delay the ripening of such fruit as grapes till the autumn when prices are better. And, in spite of cloud, Guernsey can still show a very reasonable sunshine record, especially as compared with such competing glasshouse areas as the coasts of Sussex and South Holland. Luckily this sunshine advantage (and the frost-free advantage too, though for different reasons) is most usefully marked in the late winter and spring, which is just the season when it is most valuable for bringing on flowers and tomatoes for the profitable early market. During the half-year December–May, Guernsey averages 777 hours of sunshine against 771 at Worthing and 693 in South Holland.

The 1860s were an important incubation period for Guernsey horticulture. In 1861 regular steamer services to England laid the foundations for rapid growth on all fronts. In 1864 flowers began to be sent to London markets— daffodils, gladioli, ixias and freesias in those days. Up till 1914 the variety and quantity of flowers grown continued to expand, and a flourishing bulb business was added. At that time nacissi, chrysanthemums, gladioli, carnations, sweetpeas, stocks, agapanthus, clivias and nerines were all being grown; there were 300–400 acres in cultivation and nearly $\frac{1}{2}$ million packages were being exported annually.

The flower business has seen its ups and downs since then; and, while more bulbs have been imported than exported almost every year, flowers still form an important and promising branch of horticulture. By 1965 there were about 400 acres of glass under flowers, and this area has been kept up in spite of a fall in the total glass acreage. Roses and freesias head the list these days; but many other species are grown, orchids being among the most recent and most exotic additions.

The regular steamboat services to the English markets also gave a fillip to the island's fruit business. Exports of grapes increased dramatically from 3 tons in 1855 to 50 tons in 1876 and 600 tons in 1885. The quality, however, did not keep pace with the quantity—Guernsey's grapes suffered badly from poor packing by a mass of small growers and from multiple handling on the complicated journey to market. These problems were partly solved by the 'grape case'— a primitive precursor of the present-day container—and in 1915 exports rose to a high point of 2,500 tons. The 'grape case', designed like a large squat cupboard with shelves for the fruit, provided virtually handling-free transport from grower to market; it replaced the traditional system of heaped woven baskets which had subjected the fruit to damage at every turn.

It was also in the sixties that the tomato seems to have been introduced into Guernsey; but it was quite slow to gain favour, being grown first as a catch crop in vineries and not recorded as a main crop until 1884. From about the turn of the century tomato growing went ahead famously and several vineries turned over to tomatoes. By 1913 over 10,000 tons were being exported, four or five times the weight of grape exports at the time. Subsequently tomato exports grew to 20,000 tons by 1927, 30,000 tons by 1937, 40,000 tons by 1948, and stand now around 46,000 tons. These results derive as much from improvements in methods of cultivation and marketing as from increases in acreage. The average yield per plant has risen over that period from 3lb to 8lb; in 1973 some growers topped 30lb.

In the earliest days the plants were left to wander over the ground like vegetable marrows, but were soon being trained in greenhouses. Before long the plants were plagued by disease resulting from constant use of the same soil. Early remedies involved carting in clean soil by wheelbarrow from neighbouring fields, or moving glasshouses bodily on wheels and rails to their own clean soil. In the 1920s soil sterilisation by steam replaced these methods and is still the usual prophylactic. Sterilisation obviates the constant replacement of soil, but it is expensive and time-consuming, and the labour requirements seem more onerous as wages rise. One way of avoiding this expense is to do without soil altogether; various artificial growing media have been exploited, including the use of straw bales in trenches. Perhaps the most ingenious one is the 'polythene sausage' invented and developed in the island itself. The tomatoes grow in sausage-shaped polythene bags, each big enough to support four plants, with a filling based on Irish peat, with added chemicals and, in some cases, $\frac{1}{8}$in chips of Guernsey granite. Ventilation and heating in modern glasshouses is controlled by thermostats and automatic devices for opening and shutting the vents; and carbon-dioxide is introduced to enrich the air breathed by the plants. Irrigation by overhead sprinklers is common, and more advanced houses use controlled trickle irrigation.

The earlier greenhouses were concentrated in the northern part of the island, especially in the north-east; they are still most numerous there, though they later spread to the western bays and are now to be found to some extent in every district. There is a whole range of possible explanations for the early concentration of greenhouses in the northern areas: the hours of sunshine are slightly longer there than in the south —a fact that is again being appreciated by growers; the soils tend to be lighter, warmer and easier to work; the water table is higher too, and this was especially important with early methods of growing directly in the soil. Coal was used in large quantities for inefficient heating systems, and was carried expensively by horse and cart, so that it would have been advantageous to be near St Sampson's harbour where all the coal came in. The comparative poverty of the north may have helped in two ways: people in the northern areas would be looking for new crops to cultivate while southern farmers basked in the renown and prosperity of the Guernsey herd; and immigrants from England (who took up growing in Guernsey then as Dutchmen are doing now) would find land cheaper in the north. The presence of quarrying, fishing and shipbuilding in the north-east corner may have been significant: quarrymen had free stone for building the cumbersome early greenhouses; fishermen could conveniently combine fishing with growing on small plots of land, and carpenters, made redundant with the decline in shipbuilding, would be most readily available for glass-roof carpentry near the shipyards. Technical advances first freed the industry from some of these restraints on location and made growing on parts of the southern plateau quite usual. But, since about 1930, high capital costs have meant that expansion has been mainly through extension or modernisation of existing enterprises; consequently there has been a tendency for the concentrations of that time to become more pronounced.

Today the whole horticultural industry faces a threatening future. The European demand for tomatoes has been stagnant for several years, while all the time new producers enter the industry. Competition between more and more producers for the same market becomes ever keener. In such situations the newcomer often enjoys certain advantages just by being a newcomer—new plant, new men, fresh ideas, today's location and today's business structure. The established Guernsey growers are an ageing race; in 1965 nearly three-quarters of them were already over forty years of age, and so were more than half the full-time work-force. Most of the older growers show little or no interest in improving their plant; either they hope their old glass and old methods will last them out, or they are unable to afford improvements because their glass has not been profitable enough. One reason for this is that Guernsey growers traditionally run small concerns; they are successors to the brave enterprise of the small men who pioneered the industry—small farmers putting up glass on their holdings, artisans in their backyards or on land acquired with rentes, and others having a go at growing as a spare-time money-getter. In fact, in 1970 over half the glasshouse holdings in Guernsey comprised less than 400ft of glass, which means they can only have been run as part-time enterprises; and over two-thirds of the remainder were under 800ft and must be supposed to be family enterprises unlikely to survive severe competition in future. These two categories —part-time enterprises and family enterprises—together account for just over half the total area of commercial glass in the island, while large enterprises running over 2,000ft make up a quarter of the glass but only a fortieth of the enterprises. The result is that improvement is very slow. At the present rate of progress it would take an estimated fifty-five years to renew all the island's glass.

Holland, while suffering from her own ageing glass problem, is the island's main competitor in the British tomato market. From December through April Britain is supplied almost exclusively by the Canary Islands. Tomatoes from Guernsey and Holland begin to arrive together in April, when prices are still reasonably good; they predominate in May and remain important till July, by which time prices have fallen to a third of April's. British home production leads from June to September, when Jersey field tomatoes (produced cheaply as a follow-up to new potatoes) take over at the bottom of the market.

The Dutch tomato industry is centred in the Westland— the district between The Hague and The Hook of Holland —which sports a weird glasshouse landscape uncannily reminiscent of Guernsey's own. Holland's tomato acreage is over eight times Guernsey's, although annual exports to Britain are only about the same. There remains, therefore, a vast quantity of Dutch fruit which is now sold elsewhere; but this could be directed across the Channel to Britain if

88

(right) but scallops, being unloaded here, are not so important

Page 90 (above) The fern, *Asplenium x sarniense*, a hybrid, was first discovered in the island and named in 1971; *(below left)* the giant blue echium, from the Canary Islands and rare in the other Channel Islands, dominates many gardens. Said to have been introduced to Jethou by Compton Mackenzie; *(below right)* 'ormering', or searching for this delicacy at low tides, is a favourite pastime

competition from East European countries should make conditions in the key West German market too difficult for the Dutch growers. Holland has also the advantage of a quicker sea crossing—six hours compared with ten from Guernsey—to speed the delivery of fruit and flowers to Britain, but at least the island now has roll-on roll-off facilities of its own to help save valuable hours at the docks.

FISHING

We have records of fishing in Guernsey almost as far back as we have records of anything. In the Middle Ages fishing was of capital importance to the island's economy. In 1332, of the annual revenue accruing to the Crown from the island of £1,130 8s 1d, no less than £266 13s 4d derived from fishing. The principal species caught—or at least the principal species taxed—was the conger, which is still found and caught in local waters, but it is not so highly appreciated now as then. There existed at that time a steady demand for fish to eat on fast days, and the Channel Islands were in a position to export a good part of their catch. For this purpose the fish had to be dried and salted; the salting would be done at a *salerie* and the drying on the rocks at an *éperquerie*. Several place names around the shores testify to these activities. Though both Jersey and St Malo were prominent in the fisheries of the Newfoundland Banks, there is little evidence that Guernsey seized the opportunities they offered. Instead the Guernsey fishery declined. By 1609 the *salerie de congres* was bringing the governor £6 compared with £60 200 years before.

Though the export business was dead, fishing for local needs never died out; there was a tradition of hardy islanders —often, as in Brittany, dividing their time between sea and plough—who mastered the dangerous rocky and tempestuous waters in tough traditional boats. Some of the landing places, the *cauchies*, that they used can still be seen around the island—the granite steps at Amarreurs, at Rousse, at Portelet on the west coast, and the ingenious 70° slip and winch for bringing boats straight up the rockside at La Moye. The fishermen were active in good numbers until the end of the last century, the fish market at St Peter Port often being admired by visitors—one even naming it an 'Elysium piscatorium', for the plenty and quality of its display, not to mention the cheapness of the wares. But the economies of scale overtook the Guernsey fishery, as it did others, and by the 1930s a large proportion of the fish on display had been caught by trawlers out of Hull or Grimsby and consigned to St Peter Port by the Southern Railway. Probably only the congers, mackerel, whiting and crustaceans would have been caught locally. The island's fishing industry, with its ageing practitioners, might then have expired, as many an English fishing village has done, leaving a handful of picturesque survivors to offer their services to summer visitors for trips round the Hanois or across to Herm and Jethou. However, the Guernsey fishery of today is young, keen and outward-looking—not to mention turbulent and quarrelsome at times.

The quarrels started in the 1960s. At that time the most profitable branch of fishing was potting for lobsters and crayfish, which commanded a good market both in the island and overseas. Then a number of young men, who had taken to skin-diving in the waters round the island as a sport, realised they could make a living by collecting the lobsters and crayfish direct from their habitat, thus cutting out the tedious traditional potting process. The divers were soon in conflict with the boatmen, who accused them not only of taking easy pickings from their unguarded pots but, more generally, of undermining their living and possibly the island's resources by overfishing the grounds. This was bad enough; but the divers went on to antagonise a much broader body of Guernseymen by using their techniques to harvest the sacred ormer from deep water; and they were duly accused of being responsible for the poor returns then being experienced by traditional shore-ormerers as well. Apart from a few quickly regretted scuffles, the conflict has centred mainly in the public democratic arena and the prizes contended for have been restrictions and derestrictions of fishing in this way and that way, in this area and that area. Arrests have been made and fines imposed. In 1969 a diver was fined £20 for taking ormers in a prohibited area, after being arrested by a police frogman 45ft under water off Castle Cornet. Successive States Sea Fisheries Committees have wrestled with the problem, buffeted by noisy interest groups on either side, reporting to a States trying not to be swayed by prejudice and clamour, and dogged at every turn by our basic ignorance about the habits and behaviour of the marine creatures responsible for the whole argument.

Perhaps more is known about the ormer than other crustaceans, in spite of its lesser commercial value. This large, grey, armour-clad gastropod clings to rocks between tide mark and 90ft depth. It is the centre of an established tradition in the Channel Islands, being collected, when the law allows, at low spring tides in the winter season from under stones where it lives, by eager amateurs some of whom will wade in the bitter-cold water for hours to make their catch. All islanders declare a patriotic appreciation of its flesh. A guide book of the last century declares typically, 'When beat to make it tender, and fried or stewed, it is thought to resemble a veal cutlet and is much prized'. A candid visitor of a few years later is less flattering: 'I should describe it as a hard, leathery substance, in shape a flattened oblong, with the appearance of a good-sized sea-smoothed pebble, the eating of which will inevitably bring on a fierce attack of indigestion, and possibly set up a gastritis.' The Channel Islands are at the northern limit of the ormer's natural range, and it must be in a precarious and possibly unstable environmental position, any small change in its habitat could lead in such circumstances to dramatic, in some cases possibly irreversible, changes in population.

There is an estimated stock of about 20 million ormers of all ages round the Guernsey coasts; at one time it was thought that divers might be taking as many as 750,000 mature ormers in a season, a considerable proportion. On the other hand, the catch on the shores seems to have been declining for a century; in view of this it is difficult to hold the divers solely responsible for any recent shortfall. A likely cause could well be the conduct of the shore-gatherers themselves who, in their increasing numbers, are seriously—perhaps even fatally—disturbing the habitat not only of the ormer but of the seaweed on which it feeds.

The squabbles and restrictions continue, but they seem less important than they used to because the whole fishing industry has become more enterprising and outward-looking than it was. A fish-processing plant is established at Rocquaine. The fishermen themselves have their own co-operative, with freezer, ice plant and storage on the Castle Emplacement and its own exporting vessel. For a time queen scallops were an important catch, and were exported regularly to America. Now crabs are the principal interest.

Another new venture is fish farming. Two young men have acquired a disused quarry on the north-east coast in which they propose to fatten Pacific oysters and possibly to cultivate ormers as well.

There are still over 300 boats and perhaps 600 people engaged in the island's traditional fishery, though most of them are part-timers of one kind or another. Lobsters and crayfish are still being caught and exported and the demand for them is very unlikely to diminish with time.

There was some fear that Britain's entry into the EEC might have thrown Guernsey waters open to fishermen of any of the member countries. This danger has been averted, and the present position is that Guernsey has full control of her territorial waters—that is, the sea and seabed within 3 nautical miles of the shore or of drying rocks less than 3 miles off shore—and the States legislate freely for this area; subject to this legislation any British-registered boat may fish there. Between 3 and 6 miles out, fishing is also reserved for British boats (which includes those of the Channel Islands), but if regulations are needed they are introduced by the British government. From 6 to 12 miles out the situation is the same, with the exception that the French have a right to fish for crabs and demersal fish in this belt to the westward of Guernsey as far round as a line south-west from the Etac de Serk.

LIGHT INDUSTRY

The only substantial manufacturing industry in Guernsey today dates only from 1958. The American firm of Tektronix has two oscilloscope factories on the island: in Victoria Avenue near Ivy Castle and at La Villiaze, near the airfield. Those parts not made on the spot come either by sea via Rotterdam or all the way by air from America, and the product all leaves Guernsey by air. This business is well established and well contented in Guernsey; the processes and buildings are inoffensive, and employment is provided for some 600 workers, of whom over nine-tenths are islanders.

This was the only light industry on that scale settled in the island until 1973 when Eurotherm Ltd decided to set up a plant to manufacture heat-control equipment, to employ some 200 women.

It is quite possible, though the potential profit and loss are difficult to calculate, that the fiscal inducements to encourage the setting up of businesses in the island were—during the 1960s, when none came—not as far ahead of those offered in British 'development areas' as people in Guernsey had supposed.

True to tradition, the islanders have not just sat back and

waited for readymade industries to be handed to them on a plate. Native concerns are smaller, but they are home-grown and often rooted in the soil of existing enterprise: for example, domestic glasshouses; rack and pinion gearing for operating ventilators, and irrigation diluters as spin-off from horticulture; and small-boat building as a beneficiary of the freedom of the Channel Islands from Value Added Tax.

7   COMMUNITY LIFE

NATURALLY Guernsey life was more singular in
years gone by; the visitor of a hundred years ago met a
strange language, strange customs, remains of a long
tradition of folklore, as well as a different emphasis in morals
and religion. Today, while the tendency is strong for everything to be modelled more or less closely on life in England,
there are still echoes and survivals of the island's individuality,
and an inevitable twist to such activities as education, sport
or the press, which basically do not differ widely from their
English equivalents.

THE PATOIS

You do not often hear the old Guernsey tongue nowadays,
and strangers who do are in danger of calling it 'French'. It
is related to French, of course, and derives from the same
source—Low Latin. When Latin became the usual language
of the country people of Gaul, it took on many forms. Each
village no doubt spoke slightly differently from its neighbours,
but in larger areas separate provincial dialects developed. In
the course of time the political powers, with the help of
poets and storytellers, distilled from some of these dialects
languages which could be used in administration and in
literature over wider areas. Thus, while the counts of Provence
and Toulouse along with the troubadors fashioned Provençal,
the English kings Anglo-Norman, and the kings of France

French, the country folk went on speaking their own local tongue, which usually remained unwritten and came to be referred to as *patois*. Such are the patois of the Channel Islands. As patois go they are not exceptionally archaic. They have changed through the centuries and are still changing; but they have no doubt been rather better preserved from contamination by French than most continental patois simply by being less exposed to its use in the administration and armed services.

Certain basic features of all Channel Island patois are shared with the nearer continental Norman patois, but regular differences exist between all these and French, and there are naturally variations of vocabulary as well. Some examples are given below:

French	Guernsey
toile	*tèle*
champ	*camp*
charrue	*tcherrue*
cinq	*chinq*
agneau	*agné*
puis	*pis*
lit	*lliet*

Guernsey patois differs from Jersey and Sark patois of course: Latin *mare*, the sea; Jersey *mé*; Guernsey *maïr*; and there are even variations within Guernsey, usually between the north and the south: *bel garçon* in the Low Parishes; *bàl garcin* in the High—but boundaries are not always so neat.

Guernsey proverbs illustrate the patois nicely. Some are very like proverbs elsewhere: *Chângement d'herbage est buoan pour les jânes vaux* (Young cattle need fresh grass); *I'ne faut pas faire le cottin d'vant que le viau seit naï* (Don't make the cradle before the calf is born), or *P'tit à p'tit l'ouaisé fait son nic* (A bird's nest is not made in a day). Others have a more local flavour: *Noué n'est pas Noué sans pâcrolle* (Christmas without a primrose is no Christmas);

98

Ch'est prendre de Pierre Chyvret pour dounaïr à Monsieur Careye (Robbing Chyvrer to pay Carey), and most characteristic of all, *Qui épouse Jerriais ou Jerriaise, Jamais ne vivra à son aise* (If you want a quiet life, Never take a Jersey wife).

In the nineteenth century, when the simple peasant life came to be the object of idealised admiration, obscure languages and dialects, previously left to perish or proscribed in favour of national uniformity, were sought out and encouraged. French patois received much attention in the years following Waterloo. Several patois poets wrote in Guernsey, of whom the best known were Thomas Lenfestey, Nicholas Guilbert, Georges Métivier and Denys Corbet— *le drain rimeux*, the last poet. Corbet was a great character: schoolmaster, engraver, painter (mainly of prizewinning cows), clocksmith, farmer, poet in French, English and patois. His masterpiece was an epic tour of the Guernsey of his day, *Le Touar de Guernesy*. Métivier is rated a better poet; his *Rimes guernesiais par un Catelain* date from 1831. Forty years later, when his muse was muted and fashion became more scientific, he produced the first patois dictionary. The last came out in 1967 under Marie de Garis.

Guernsey patois has been in decline for a long time. English had entered the States by the end of the last century, and was taken on by the schools in the early 1900s. In 1966 about 7,000–10,000 people could still speak some patois— according to a 2 per cent sample survey of country households —while 2,000–3,000 regarded it as their everyday language. The patois is best preserved in the country districts farthest from St Peter Port. Around Rocquaine Bay there are patois speakers in nine out of ten families, while the east coast is almost entirely anglicised.

CUSTOMS AND CELEBRATIONS

In the old days, people laboured long, long hours; but work

GUERNSEY

was enlivened on special occasions by jollifications and there were times which called for celebration. The collection of vraic from the seashore, for instance, a vital part of traditional farming, was always accompanied by some kind of rustic picnic as well as by orming and congering, and finished traditionally with a ducking usually of a female of the party. Picnics also accompanied the shared use of *la grand' querrue*, the great plough, used in cultivation for parsnips.

Certain days of the year used to be marked by special observances: on Shrove Tuesday, pancakes as in England; on Good Friday, limpets baked on rocks by the seashore; on the first Sunday in Lent, brandons—bonfires from which burning straw was carried round the neighbourhood. The goings-on at this time in Alderney are mentioned by every writer, but never circumstantially enough to satisfy modern curiosity. Guernsey seems to have been well behaved by comparison. On New Year's Eve the boys dressed up a 'guy' —a log or something of the kind—known as the 'budloe' (?*bout de l'an*), which they carried round in a funeral procession, holding turnip lanterns and begging *hivrières* (winter presents). The boys then burnt him on a bonfire; the Big Budloe was burnt at Galet Heaume. While the boys were disposing of the budloe, their elders have for centuries spent the day in meeting and greeting, and in consuming *gâches à corinthes*—Guernsey cakes with raisins. With the bean-jar and pork hock, the gâche is a speciality of the Guernsey cuisine: rub 1lb of Guernsey butter in 3lb of flour. Mix 1oz yeast with a little water to blood heat. Add to the flour and let it rise. Add 1½lb sultanas or currants, candied peel, yolk of an egg with a little more warm water and beat the dough with the hand till it leaves the hand clean. Leave to rise for 2 hours; put in a greased tin and bake in a moderate oven.

The most popular form of entertainment was for neighbours or relatives to gather in the evening at the house of one of them, bringing their knitting, sitting round by the

100

light of a single cresset lamp telling tales, singing songs, playing word games. On the more formal occasions the young people would sit on the floor, the men on stools, and the matrons on the green bed. When the young were the centre of the party, they were more likely to share the green bed themselves, leading sometimes to some anxiety among their elders. This green bed, *le lit de fouaille* or *la joncquière*, was an established Channel Island institution. It probably evolved from the pile of furze fuel kept in early times near the fire, which could be made a more comfortable resting place by covering it with haulms of bracken, rushes or peas. Later, carpentry frames were made for the green bed, which continued to stand in the corner of every rustic kitchen up to World War I. Only about five dozen green beds survive now; many are in attics, though some three dozen are declared to be still in use. On high occasions the green bed would be decorated and garlanded with flowers, and at midsummer the effigy of *la môme* would be seated on it and receive homage.

THE OLD GODS

The old times, before Christianity, are not quite forgotten in Guernsey, and their memory was greener still in the traditional society of the last century. Midsummer, which is the big bonfire season of northern Europe, was in Guernsey an occasion for dancing—in places sacred to the old gods:

> *J'irons tous à la Saint-Jean*
> *Dansair sus la Rocque Balan*

All the stones of ancient times were objects of fear and wonder, and bad luck was supposed to attend anyone who interfered with them. That has not, however, prevented most of them from disappearing in the course of time.

Fairies and goblins were plentiful in Guernsey, but they seem to have been very similar to their kind elsewhere. Witches, on the other hand, flourished exceedingly. Between

1550 and 1650, witches tried in Guernsey numbered 103, of whom 47 were executed and 32 banished. This compares with about 1,000 such trials in England, then certainly over ten times more populous. Guernsey was a witch-hunting country in those days, fit to compare perhaps with New England rather than with the old. This predilection may have been related to the triumph of Puritanism, or perhaps to the cut-off and ingrown state of island society as a whole. Under these circumstances private grudges can fester and find welcome relief in denunciations—perhaps those who informed the Germans of their neighbours' wireless sets during the Occupation followed the same tradition. A genuine belief in witchcraft survived amazingly late in Guernsey. In 1912 children at St Peter's in the Woods school, when found to be lousy, were alleged to be bewitched; and in 1914 a woman in St Sampson's was imprisoned for eight days on a charge of disorderly conduct for selling charms against witchcraft. She had declared a metal box, possessed by a neighbour, to be 'full of little devils', and had directed this neighbour to bury secretly packets containing Brown and Polson's flour, Paisley flour, brown starch, salt and baking powder. No more recent cases are known.

THE COMING OF CHRISTIANITY

The conversion of Guernsey is traditionally ascribed to St Sampson and St Magloire, Welshmen who came over from Brittany in the middle of the sixth century. Though based solely on tradition, the story has the ring of truth, at least in outline. The sixth century was part of the great missionary period of the Celtic churches, and ties were then close between Brittany and Wales—and indeed Cornwall and Ireland too. The Celtic Sea had real meaning then. When the Church in Guernsey emerges from the mists, however, it is already in the Roman communion and organised on

Roman lines. There are already the ten parishes we know today—probably based on pre-conversion settlements. The island lay in the diocese of Coutances and the province of Rouen, and had its own rural dean. Monastic life was also closely linked with France; land was held by the Norman monasteries of Mont St Michel, Blanchelande, Cherbourg, Marmoutier and Caen; and the island communities at the Vale, Martinvast, Lihou and Herm all derived from French houses.

Political separation from Normandy in 1204 had no immediate effect on spiritual life, though the monastic link with 'alien' houses was broken by Henry V. Bulls of Alexander VI to transfer the Channel Islands from Coutances to Salisbury and later to Winchester remained dead letters. Coutances carried on as before. More curious still, Henry VIII's Reformation itself had no effect on this situation. The French Roman Catholic bishop continued to function for many years after Henry had become Head of the Church of England, and there is even a brief on record in which the king reminds the bishop that in the islands he exercises his jurisdiction as the king's officer and not the pope's. Of course this could not last, and Elizabeth I eventually extinguished the jurisdiction of Coutances by Order in Council in 1569, attaching Guernsey to the distant see of Winchester. Winchester was so distant in fact that the deans of Guernsey and Jersey enjoyed, and still enjoy, a degree of autonomy known elsewhere only to a handful of peculiars. The dean is a kind of chancellor and archdeacon combined, and appeals from his court go to the bishop alone.

Guernsey did not come through the Reformation unscathed by the fanaticism of the times. Suspected papists were flogged through the streets of St Peter Port under Elizabeth I; but that was mild when compared with the reign before. In 1556 a mother and her two daughters were convicted of heresy by the Ecclesiastical Court and condemned by the Royal Court to be burned at the stake. Heylin's account makes it plain that they were humanely though inefficiently strangled before burning; but a very different circumstance has made this execution memorable for horror ever since. It is reported that when actually at the stake and surrounded by flames one of the daughters gave birth to a boy. The infant was rescued and carried to the bailiff, who ordered it to be flung back into the flames. 'So that pretty babe was born a martyr, and added to the holy innocents,' concludes Heylin—though some are unconvinced of the authenticity of the tale.

The Church of England

In spite of its firmness with Coutances, the Crown failed to bring Guernsey into line with English practice for a further century. The Church of England could provide no French-speaking pastors and the island was supplied instead from continental sources, especially from Geneva, where the exiled Protestant bailiff, William de Beauvoir, became deacon of Knox and Coverdale's English church and persuaded Calvin to send Nicholas Baudouin and others to his native island. These Presbyterian ministers were no men to submit to deans or bishops. With the collaboration of the Puritan governor they set up a full Presbyterian ecclesiastical system in Guernsey. For each parish there was a consistory of elders and deacons, for Guernsey a colloque, and for the Channel Islands an annual synod. All ceremonies that smelt even faintly of popery were proscribed; public penance and pastors' admonitions were the rule; and Sundays became devoted to compulsory churchgoing.

It is not surprising that Guernsey was strong for Parliament in the Civil War, nor that the Church of England used the Restoration as the occasion for establishing itself in the island. Calvinism, however, died hard in some ways. At St Saviour's church, for instance, until the middle of the nineteenth century, the Sanctuary remained in a side chapel with pews in a square facing it, and communions were confined to Christmas, Easter, Whitsun and Michaelmas, when the people all came dressed in black and the church was decorated with evergreens. Until early in the century the metrical psalms were sung by the congregation seated, and baptisms were performed at the altar for want of fonts.

Nowadays the Church of England in Guernsey looks, except for its dean, much like the Church in any comparable part of England. There are ten rectors, each with his parish, as there have always been; and, in addition, five vicars with parishes carved from the largest of the ten: Holy Trinity, St James the Less, St John the Evangelist and St Stephen from St Peter Port, and St Matthew from St Mary of the Castel.

The Methodists

Methodism had a hard time of it at first; it may have been the Puritan tradition which made it so widely accepted in the long run. The first to preach in Guernsey (1783) was the famous 'Squire' Brackenbury, whose main field at the time was Jersey. From Jersey as well, two years later, came the first regular missionary, young John de Quetteville, himself a Jerseyman. 'I was very seasick,' he wrote of his journey, 'I thought, all goes well, I am beginning to bear my cross.' He was joined the following year by Adam Clarke, who gave his impression of the first meeting he attended: 'I have never seen such disorder and confusion in the worst parts of Norfolk or of Cornwall'—the disorder and confusion arose from the opposition, of course, not from the faithful.

The highlight of the missionary era was the visit in 1787 of John Wesley himself, then in his eighty-fifth year. Wesley preached almost incessantly for four days and, on leaving, was forced back to Guernsey by no doubt providential winds for a further week, which he spent in preaching as well. He also found time for half an hour with the lieutenant-governor and was asked to dinner later. In spite of this social recognition the Methodists faced abuse and ill treatment for years to come. Attempts to have them banished failed, however, and when they built their first chapel in rue Le Marchant, the bailiff and his wife contributed £50. The second chapel did not come till 1814 but thereafter chapels came thick and fast, and by 1835 there were at least thirteen. Unfortunately most of the early ones were abandoned or rebuilt later, and those now to be seen in every corner of the island date from the second half of the last century and are not much to today's artistic taste.

By the time of the Centenary there were 44 chapels, 16 ministers, 78 local preachers and 48 Sunday Schools, with 1,300 teachers and 5,000 in attendance. It is estimated that every other Protestant in Guernsey was a Methodist of some sort—for the Wesleyans, in addition to being divided into French and English congregations, were diversified over the years by Bible Christians, Primitive Methodists and the New Connexion. In 1932 there was a grand re-union of all Methodists; but membership remained stationary between 2,000 and 2,500 in a constantly rising island population. Today registered membership for the bailiwick stands at rather over 2,750, but adherents are said to number over twice as many. There are two circuits, with ten regular ministers and five supernumeraries, and 22 Sunday Schools.

Roman Catholics

The Roman Catholics came back to Guernsey with the émigrés from Revolutionary France, two mission priests being appointed in 1802. By 1829 a chapel had been built in Burnt Lane; and by 1850 St Joseph's Church, where Cardinal Wiseman himself came over to preach a year later. His reception was reminiscent of Methodist experience half a century before. As he drove to church, the windows of his coach were broken by a howling mob. At St Joseph's 'A crowd of Protestants came to hear him, and the English directness and

Page 107 (above) Experimental oyster farm in Noirmont Quarry; (below) St Saviour's reservoir in 1971 demonstrates the water supply problem

Page 108 (above) When quarrying was once an island industry in the northern parishes, and stone for road metalling was an important export; (below) the West Quay before the harbours were rebuilt in Victorian times. The main town drain is on the left

common sense of his discourse so won upon them that a complete revulsion took place. The Cardinal ended by staying several days, making friends with many of the islanders and dining with the Lieutenant-governor.' Now there are three Roman Catholic parishes and three chapels, and the Salesian Brothers, Presentation Sisters, Nuns of the Sacred Heart and Hospitallers of the Holy Sepulchre all work in the island.

The unquestioned crown of Guernsey schooling is the college founded by Queen Elizabeth I in 1563. The college was provided with land in the Grange which it still occupies; with an excellent master in Adrian Saravia, later one of the translators of King James' bible, and with statutes enjoining instruction in the Latin and Greek tongues, though the master was allowed to 'occasionally add something of his own, and by a variety of exercises sharpen the wits of the scholars, and even remit something of these and concede some intermission for singing, arithmetic, writing, and also, but seldom, for play'.

The school went through a bad patch of neglect and nepotism in the eighteenth century and had to be practically re-founded in 1824. Two years later, when the foundation stone of the present buildings was laid, the ceremony was as magnificent as the island could make it, and the subsequent refreshments as finely graded as the society that conceived them. The boys were 'regaled in a most splendid manner under marquees'. The Royal Court, a part of the clergy, Directors of the College, and the Militia Officers dined together at Rosetti's Assembly Rooms. The douzeniers from the country parishes dined together at Cole's Hotel. Wine and biscuits were distributed to the troops upon the New Ground. And the workmen were presented by the Royal Court with a good solid dinner and a hogshead of wine.

From that time Elizabeth College became for many years more or less another English Victorian army-class public school; but during the present century it has become much more closely identified with the island and nowadays draws most of its 600 pupils from Guernsey itself.

Guernsey girls had to wait till 1872 for their public school. The Ladies' College was very much a child of the times, starting under the superintendence of a pupil of the great Miss Beale of Cheltenham. It flourished in converted and extended premises in the Grange till 1963 when it moved out to a new site at Melrose.

There was a parish school in St Peter Port in 1513; in St Martin's and St Peter's in the Woods almost as early, and in the Castel by the seventeenth century. The last parishes got theirs at the beginning of the nineteenth century. Compulsory education came late, in 1900, and even then was effective only up to the fourth grade. School-leaving age was not raised to 13–14 until 1935; it rose to 15 in 1963. The older pupils were provided with what were long known as the Inter-mediate Schools, and after World War II the States provided grants for those going on to university in England.

Nowadays, educational opportunities and provision are remarkably similar to those in England, though with little call for comprehensive schooling. There is a thorough free education system until fifteen years of age, with medical care and all trimmings, scholarships for higher education, further education classes, a college of further education, and provision for 'special education' and for sub-normals. Blind and deaf children are sent to schools in England, their numbers being too few to justify provision for them in the island.

LIBRARIES AND MUSEUMS

Although there is no library founded or supported by the States of Guernsey, there are two private foundations. The

Guille-Allès Library, above the French Halles, occupies premises which served originally as the Assembly Rooms; it also has a small museum. Guille and Allès were contemporaries who both returned to their native island after making good overseas. Guille founded a library in 1856; in 1882 he was joined by Allès, and together they moved into the present premises and absorbed the pre-existing Mechanics' Institute.

The Priaulx Library, dating from 1889, occupies the house of de B. Priaulx, its benefactor, in a beautiful position at the head of the peaceful Candie Gardens, one of the most attractive spots in all St Peter Port.

Guernsey's principal museum collection is being housed in a building in Candie Gardens. The collection has developed in all directions from a germ in the collections of the famous Lukis family of amateur but formidably 'professional' archaeologists, great diggers in their day and careful and thorough in their records long before the same could be said of most of their kind.

The Folk Museum is accommodated in the old stables at Saumarez Park. The *pièces de résistance* are a reconstructed old Guernsey kitchen and the augmented Walter Langlois collection of farm implements.

The Occupation Museum, which grew from the enthusiasm of a schoolboy, Richard Heaume, who started it in a loft on his family farm at Les Houards, Forest, is now the responsibility of the Guernsey Occupation Society.

The Militia Museum occupies suitably warlike quarters in Castle Cornet.

SPORT

All kinds of sport seem to flourish in the island, from badminton to boxing, and from netball to softball (champions of Britain 1974). Water sports are naturally very popular, though Guernsey here veers rather towards widespread

111

participation than to competitive prowess—as, for instance, in the Castle Swim, across Havelet Bay, or the Herm Swim. Again, while there are eights, fours, and single rowing events, the one that hits the headlines is the tough, seamanlike Sark to Jersey Row.

Messing about in boats is universal. There are two local clubs, the Guernsey Yacht Club, and the dignified blue-ensign Royal Channel Islands Yacht Club. Three marinas have been created in recent years, all in imaginative ways. Disused Beaucette Quarry was opened up to the sea by the simple expedient of inviting the Royal Engineers to blow through the narrow neck of rock between the quarry and the sea; the original harbour of Guernsey—the Old Harbour of St Peter Port—was converted to a yacht basin by building a sill at the mouth to retain the water of the tide; the same procedure was adopted with the Albert Dock, a section of the New Harbour which was meant to become the island's dry dock but never made it.

The most popular game of all is football, and particularly the competition for the Muratti Vase. This is an inter-island event, between Guernsey, Jersey, and Alderney, which combines the drama of international contest with the intimacy of local league football. It inspires an enthusiasm unequalled in island sport, and achieves the feat of taking a crowd of Guernseymen to Jersey and a crowd of Jerseymen to Guernsey every year, and even more remarkably each crowd enjoys the experience—if their team wins. Alderney has only won the competition once since the presentation of the Vase in 1905, but soldiers on partly because Alderney people are like that, and partly because all well-conditioned big-islanders enjoy an excuse for a visit to Alderney.

In 1970 Guernsey first entered real international sport by sending a team to the Commonwealth Games at Edinburgh. For the second appearance at the Games, this time at Christchurch, Guernsey's team included three walkers, one runner, three lawn-bowlers and a strong shooting contingent comprising full-bore, small-bore and pistol contingents. Guernsey's strength in competitive shooting is nothing new; it goes back to the days of the Island Militia, when proficiency in shooting was every man's duty and excellence was encouraged by precept and example.

Outdoor sport does not do too badly for space in Guernsey considering the size of the community, and indoor sport is fortunate in acquiring a purpose-built Indoor Sports Centre at Beauséjour high above St Peter Port.

ENTERTAINMENT

While the islanders enjoyed their traditional festivities, 'persons of quality' were attending the dances at the Assembly Rooms, which flourished from 200 to 100 years ago. A high point on the social calendar until World War II was the Sovereign's Official Birthday parade of the militia and garrison at Fort George, which everyone turned out to watch, making it very much an island occasion.

Nowadays entertainment in Guernsey is pretty much what it is in a provincial place of comparable size in England. There are discos, cinemas, the Little Theatre, dances and bars—though it is hard to find anything quite equivalent to the English pub. The *cabarets* of former times were looked upon as low places and some of this attitude seems to have persisted as many islanders prefer to drink in the bars of hotels.

THE MEDIA

The press

There is evidence to suggest that books were printed in Guernsey in the sixteenth century. Walsingham mentions in correspondence a French version of the Book of Common Prayer; but no copies of it survive. By 1776 one Rognon

113

printed a *Recueil de Maximes, de Pensées et de Refléxions*, and the presses hummed from then on, fostering before long Thomas de la Rue, one of the island's more illustrious émigré sons.

The first newspaper was the *Gazette de l'Ile de Guernesey*, which had an exceptionally long life. Starting in 1789–91, it changed name in 1842 to *La Gazette Officielle*, became a kind of local *London Gazette*, and expired in 1934 with under a hundred subscribers.

During the intervening years there have been twenty-nine newspapers that survived over twelve months, besides many almost literally ephemeral effusions, in both French and English. At present *The Guernsey Press*—founded in 1896 as *The Evening Press*—is the island's only paper. It has a daily circulation of some 15,000, and is deeply involved with every aspect of island life. If it pays little attention to events farther afield, it is only following the general trend of the British provincial evening press. The London papers are easily available and widely read in Guernsey; between them the dailies, evenings and Sundays have a circulation of nearly ½ million a week at a cost in chartered planes of hundreds of pounds a day.

Television

Guernsey shares with Jersey one of Europe's smallest television stations: 'Channel', which has rather more than 35,000 viewers. The result of 'Channel', so far as the islands are concerned, is exactly opposite to the effect of the press. Whereas Jersey and Guernsey newspapers rarely mention the other island, except from time to time as sports opponents, 'Channel' is a joint venture through and through, and anyone who wants to view Guernsey events has to sit through Jersey events as well.

GUERNSEY SOCIETIES

'This barbarous people hate letters' wrote Adrian Saravia in the reign of Queen Elizabeth I; his words could scarcely be repeated in Queen Elizabeth II's. Nowadays not only letters but every form of polite learning flourishes in the island.

The doyen of the learned bodies is La Société Guernesiaise. A typical child of the Victorian enthusiasm for earnest improvement, La Société was founded in 1882 by a small band of naturalists as the Guernsey Natural Science Society. The first president was Sir E. McCulloch, statesman (later bailiff), naturalist, and the greatest collector of island folk lore; while H. M. Gwatkin, a founding committee member, was a nationally famous naturalist with a special interest in the palates of sea snails. The name 'Société Guernesiaise' was taken in 1922, and signalised a widening of interest to include every aspect of the study of Guernsey. There are sections specialising in conservation, astronomy, geology, geography, botany, zoology, ornithology, entomology, archaeology, history, industrial archaeology, and philology. Membership is nowadays about 800. Every year, except during the Occupation, the society has, with unfailing diligence, published its Reports and Transactions. These cover a great variety of topics which together form an essential background to understanding the island in depth.

The other societies include L'Assemblaie d'Guernesiais, which seeks to study and keep alive the native language and folkways of the island; the National Trust of Guernsey, with aims similar to those of the National Trusts in Britain, and the Guernsey Society, an association for islanders living outside Guernsey, for whom it publishes a quarterly review.

8   AN ISLAND RESORT

WHETHER the visitor arrives by sea or by air the
fact that Guernsey is an island is borne in on him
straight away. The air passenger, if he is lucky,
sees the whole landscape of Guernsey laid out before him—
the acres of glass that crowd the northern end glittering in
the sun like the marble sarcophagi of some immense and
opulent Mediterranean cemetery. As the plane flies over the
southern plateau, a rocky and sometimes spumy seacoast can
be observed, followed by a mosaic of bright green little fields
separated by darker hedgerows and peppered with red roofs,
and again the inevitable glasshouses. The traveller by sea
enjoys the incomparable arrival at St Peter Port, an experience whose praises have been sung—and with reason—by
practically every writer on Guernsey. For the visitor from
England it is a voyage of islands, an unfolding of insularity.
First the Casquets, barely emerging from the waves, with
Alderney a long low detached form to port. As the destination
comes nearer, Sark, Herm and Jethou sort themselves out
from the mainland of Guernsey, and Jersey can be discerned
in the distance. A whole archipelago, with Guernsey its hub.
And Guernsey has all the charm and mystery and concentration of interest common in islands. It is also a special
island. First it is a Channel Island, and the Channel Islands
as a whole enjoy a privileged position as English territory in
a French setting and a French latitude. Inglis put it neatly

116

as early as 1835: 'There is one advantage which Jersey possesses over all continental places. It is more English. English comfort is better understood in it, English ways more common.' And since his day the Englishness has not ceased to increase, in Guernsey as well as in Jersey, so that the visitor from England can always feel at home. Increasing numbers of French visitors too are finding their way across the sea nowadays, and for them *le Bobby* and *'Vive la Reine'* are a big draw. The French can thus go abroad while almost staying at home; and the English can stay at home while going abroad.

Guernsey is just the right size too. Some islands are so tiny that there is only one village or town, only one place to stay. Alderney is like that. Some are big enough to be simply the frame for a number of separate resorts. The Isle of Wight comes immediately to mind; visitors may tour the island, but each resort is a self-contained entity with its own hotels, beaches, amusements and life, just as if it was on the mainland. Guernsey lies between these extremes. There are no separate 'resorts' on the island. When visitors go home, they say they have been to Guernsey, not to St Peter Port or Pleinmont or St Martin's. While on holiday they look upon the whole island as their oyster. The cheapness of hire-cars, the profusion of buses, the shortness of the distances make movement from hotel to beach—choosing the best for each day's wind—to town, to country pubs, to beauty spots, an easy matter from every corner of the island. At the same time Guernsey is not so small that the visitor has no choice left. There is room in town, room in the suburbs, room in the country; on the seacoast and inland; in the south and in the west. Such a balanced island resort is in reality quite a rarity.

EARLY VISITORS

The introduction of the cross-Channel steamers in the nineteenth century led to a great increase in the number of visitors to the island. So long as communications between England and Guernsey depended upon the vagaries of the wind, few had undertaken the chancy voyage unless they were obliged to for business or personal reasons. But the fast and regular steamship services opened up the island to other travellers and a thin but significant trickle of them arrived each summer.

There is little record from the pens of the visitors themselves how they spent their time in Guernsey, but the early books written for their use are all serious and compendious. They say little of the picturesque or the sublime, but much of the state of agriculture and trade, and even more in proportion of the intricacies and peculiarities of government. Obviously the earliest visitors were earnest and enquiring folk, but they were concerned with sightseeing as well. They duly 'did' all the public buildings in the town, observing especially the markets and the new promenades and harbour works. The suburbs came in for special notice, the taste and unpretentious opulence of the new quarters in The Grange elicited praise, as did the standard of gardening which was already a feature of Guernsey life.

The charms of the rest of the island were also appreciated. Inglis wrote in 1835: 'To one visiting Guernsey, I would offer the same advice as I did when speaking of Jersey. Visit whatever may be pointed out; but undertake at all events a pedestrian journey round the island. Descend into the bays, double the headlands, and skirt the cliffs, though it may be necessary to hold by the furze. This is the way to see an island.'

By the middle of the century the quest for the picturesque was becoming more insistent. Rooke, writing in 1856, entitled his guide *The Channel Islands, pictorial, legendary and descriptive*. The view from Vale Castle is described in a way scarcely possible today '. . . beyond the port stands the old church . . . most picturesquely situate, the undulating coast-line stretches far away, and in the distance is the town. Islands, shipping, and rocks complete the seaview; while inland the tall windmills wave their arms above the fields supplying the rich food for those mighty giants. Immediately beneath, a fair valley, with rich green grass, well dotted with the far famed cows of Guernsey, extends across the island . . .'

The impressionist painter Renoir, who came to Guernsey on a working holiday in the autumn of 1883, accompanied by his wife and Paul Lhote, was enchanted by the landscape: 'What a pretty little place! What pretty paths! Superb cliffs, beaches such as Robinson Crusoe must have had on his island!' The people enchanted him no less: 'Nothing is more amusing, wandering among the rocks than to surprise young girls in the process of getting ready for a swim; they, although English, are not otherwise frightened away.' Moulin Huet was obviously his favourite sketching ground. His holiday yielded eighteen pictures, counting finished canvases and sketches worked up later—sometimes with the incorporation of such incongruous features as white chalk cliffs. One of these paintings, entitled 'Cradle Rock', is in the National Gallery; one is in the Louvre; the remainder in America or in private collections.

For seeing the countryside the most popular method was the Island Tour. The leisurely perambulations behind sturdy Guernsey horses always started and finished in town; but at fixed points on the routes stops were made at which the ladies and gentlemen combined admiration of the landscape with partaking of refreshment. These stopping places gave rise to a number of establishments adapted to the purpose, some specially built, some converted from alehouses; the most notable were at L'Erée, Le Gouffre, Petit Bôt, Cobo, Pleinmont and St Martin's (Queen's). From these modest beginnings, the first regular country hotels were to grow at a later date, but in the mid-nineteenth century visitors stayed in St Peter Port which had the only suitable accommodation. The guidebooks have a good deal to say of the ins and outs of local society, though it is doubtful if many visitors saw much of it. Perhaps the permanent residents, who had already come to Guernsey for the cheapness of living there, found this information more valuable.

Among those in residence in the town in the 1860s was Victor Hugo, already a famous man of letters when he was exiled from France by Napoleon III. It was in Guernsey that Hugo wrote eight of his major works, including his greatest *Les Misérables*; the first series of *La Légende des Siècles*, and of course *Les Travailleurs de la Mer*, which is set in the Channel Islands—though Guernsey opinion was that it did not reflect an intimate understanding of island life. On his arrival Hugo bought a twenty-three-room house in Hauteville, an aristocratic suburban quarter of the town. His heirs subsequently presented the house to the City of Paris, which has taken pains to keep the place as it was when Hugo lived in it—a kind of museum of his fifteen years in Guernsey. And a remarkable museum it makes. Hugo transformed everything he touched and La Maison Victor Hugo is every inch his creation in all except the bare walls. Hugo's life in Guernsey was mainly a family affair. He rose about six, worked all forenoon, stripped for a rub with cold water at eleven, dined at twelve en famille, and often walked afterwards with his mistress, Juliette Drouet, who was established in a house opposite his own. He knew some of the local men of literature—Georges Métivier, for example—but did not mix much in island society. More to his taste was the dinner for poor children which he gave every Thursday of his last seven years. Even after Hugo was free to live in France, he came back to his house in Hauteville, firstly to write *Quatre-vingt-treize*, his first considerable work after the end of his exile, and later for recuperation from illness and fatigue.

AN ISLAND RESORT

DEVELOPMENT OF TOURISM

In the 1920s and 1930s two innovations combined to disrupt the earlier pattern of life for the visitor to Guernsey—the beach and the motorbus. The cult of the beach alone might have led to an abandonment of the town and a concentration of hotels on and near the best parts of the coastline. But the motorbus came to the town's rescue. It killed the old-style leisurely charabanc tour, but at the same time, by putting every part of the island within quick and easy reach, it made it an attractive possibility to stay in town and travel out every fine day to an appropriate beach. In spite of this, hotels and guest houses began to develop in force outside town; by the end of the 1930s nearly half the island's accommodation was in the country parishes, mostly within easy reach of the coast and mainly close to the south-east corner which combined the most attractive beaches with the best cliff scenery. The history of almost all these hotels is much the same. They grew up from humble roots, converted from private houses, and adding bits and pieces as demand and available funds dictated—genuine examples of Guernsey self-help. The 'Manor House' at Petit Bôt, for example, was converted in 1932 into a simple ten-bedroom hotel without electricity, gas or mains water. In 1934 all services were introduced; by 1939 there were forty bedrooms; now there are fifty-six and improvements in appointments are being made all the time.

The period since World War II has been one of dramatic expansion. Whereas between 1920 and 1938 the number of arrivals in the island increased only from 50,000 to 70,000, by 1975 they had reached 300,000. All these additional visitors had travelled by air. The flight from Britain is not only quicker than the sea crossing, it can start from many more places. The cross-Channel boats from Weymouth tap the south coast and in part the London market, while the airborne visitors can set off from the Midlands, Wales, even Scotland.

Hotel and boarding house accommodation shows a similar expansion; available beds rose from 5,500 in 1951 to 12,500 in 1975. And no doubt they are better beds too. The States established a tight control over visitors' accommodation in 1946, and their grading system has helped to raise standards. Even in the last decade low-grade accommodation has fallen from over a third to under a sixth of the whole.

TOURIST TRENDS

After the last war there set in all over the western world a swing in taste away from the picturesque, well clothed and vegetated scene to more open, harsher, barer landscape, a swing that has led from the dripping Alpine ravine to the open sunny skislope, from the Italian lakes to the Greek isles, from snug caves to open, breezy suntanning beaches. In Guernsey it is true that the breezes are more often of the kind that the visitor would rather take cover from; but in holiday preferences Hope and Fashion are levers, and even in Guernsey there could be discerned during those years a trend, if not away from the traditional snug bays and cliffs of the south and east, at least towards the low, spacious, skylit bays of the west and north. But the west coast of Guernsey is no Cycladean islet; it is closely built up with glasshouses; it is followed by one of the principal main roads of an island gorged with traffic—whatever may be said for its beaches, it is scarcely an ideal place to stay, but, thanks to the hire-car, the area can be visited quite easily by day. Just as the motorbus saved St Peter Port as a town for visitors in the 1920s, so the hire-car led to a modest development in the Guernsey countryside in the 1950s and 1960s.

Here and there, in what remains of that delectable landscape over which the early visitors rambled, old houses have been converted into country hotels where today's tourists can enjoy some of the quiet that used to reign all over Guernsey, with the freedom to motor to other parts of the island by day and in the evenings in a manner quite impossible in former times.

9   ADMINISTRATION AND THE LAW

IN the early years of the tenth century, a band of North-men under one Rollo made themselves masters of the lower valley of the Seine. The king of France, Charles the Simple, was forced to make the best of a fait accompli. He met Rollo at Clair sur Epte on the border of their territories in 911 and there executed a treaty with him which had the effect of establishing Rollo in legitimate possession of his territory, but with the formal standing of a duke owing feudal allegiance to the king of France as his overlord. The Channel Islands were not included in Rollo's duchy; but by 933 the Norman dukes had extended their bounds to cover practically all that is known as Normandy today, including the islands.

Guernsey and Normandy

Although the dukes were technically subject to the kings of France, in fact they ruled Normandy as independent sovereigns, building up a well-governed and powerful little state, with its own administration, law, customs, and policy. Within a century the Norman dukes were ready for the next step, the conquest of England. After 1066, while the Norman

Page 125 (above) One of Guernsey's two surviving passage graves. This one is at Le Creux ès Faïes on the west coast; *(below)* pepperbox fort at L'Ancresse Common in the north, one of the many built during the Napoleonic wars

Page 126 People: *(top left)* Guernseys are still knitted in the traditional manner by the fireside; *(top right)* Major A. G. ('Peter') Wood became tenant of Herm in 1949 and the island prospered; *(left)* Victor Hugo lived in exile in Guernsey 1854–1870 and Guernsey is the scene of his novel, *Toilers of Sea*

rulers were sovereign kings of England, without overlords, Normandy remained a part of France and the dukes were still vassals of the French king in respect of it. As time went by they inherited by marriage additional lands in France, Brittany, Anjou, Touraine, Maine and the vast Duchy of Aquitaine, all of which remained also technically part of the French kingdom. So long as the Norman kings of England remained strong and resolute, they were able to make theirs the effective rule over all these wide possessions, which together covered more of France than the French kings themselves controlled.

This was an unstable balance of forces. It might be upset by the coincidence of weakness on the throne of England and strength on that of France. And so it happened at the end of the twelfth century. England was enfeebled by the continual absences of Richard I, while French policy was in the capable and determined hands of Philip Augustus. The early death of Richard further weakened the English kings, leading to rivalry between his successor, John, and Arthur, the son of his elder brother Geoffrey. Petty hostilities between John and Philip became frequent, Philip exploiting the cause of Arthur and other malcontents, as he had earlier that of Richard and John against their father Henry II. In 1200 John won the enmity of the powerful house of Lusignan by marrying Isabelle of Angoulême who was already betrothed to a Lusignan. The Lusignans appealed to Philip, who summoned John as Duke of Aquitaine (the Lusignans' homeland) to appear before his court. John refused, and was condemned in 1202 to the forfeiture of all his fiefs held of the French crown, Normandy not excluded. King Philip was as good as his word. Within two years Rouen had been taken and the whole of Normandy was in his hands—all that is, except the Channel Islands, for Philip was too weak by sea to hold them.

The islands were now left in a thoroughly anomalous

H   127 position. They had formed part of the Duchy of Normandy, whose duke had recently forfeited his duchy by judgment of the French court. Like the rest of Normandy, they had never formed part of the kingdom of England, but always of the kingdom of France. John still claimed Normandy as rightfully his, and from his point of view the islands were simply a part of his rightful inheritance. But since 1259, when by the Treaty of Paris Henry III formally surrendered his claim to the duchy of Normandy, it has been impossible even to pretend that the kings and queens of England rule in the Channel Islands 'as Dukes of Normandy'.

Guernsey and England

As a matter of practical politics an entirely new situation was created in 1204, a situation which is today virtually unaltered. The Channel Islands form a part of the dominions of the kings of England, but no part of the kingdom of England; and this political situation has ever since 1204 been the basic condition of life in the islands—even more so in the last hundred years than at any time before.

This strange partnership has never been an easy one between these half dozen small islands off the coast of France and the fully fledged realm of England, later to grow into the United Kingdom and become the metropolis of a world-wide empire. A great deal has been achieved by the exercise of the very English art of not defining anything too closely, always leaving a little give at the joints, and not pushing any disagreement to its logical conclusion. The position of the islanders has been perfectly expressed by a distinguished Guernseyman: 'The islanders, as always, were trying to have it both ways—to be English when it was a question of paying customs, to be Norman when they wanted to be independent.' On the whole over the centuries the islanders have not only been trying to have it both ways; they have succeeded in having it both ways.

128

In the three centuries after 1204 the islands were a useful possession for an England constantly at war with France, and so the kings treated the islands carefully, respected their separateness on the whole, and granted them the valuable and important right of trading with England as if they were English, and this right has been the cornerstone of their economic life ever since then. So long as kings were kings a personal union such as that between England and the Channel Islands was a logical, workable, and indeed a common, arrangement. The king could deal with English business in the morning and Guernsey business in the afternoon, taking the counsel of whomsoever he chose but making the decisions in each case himself. The rub came when the king became 'the Crown', simply a fictional executive for the decisions of ministers responsible to a representative parliamentary assembly. When the Crown has also other subjects, who are not represented in the parliament, this situation becomes difficult. The American colonies revolted over just that issue in the eighteenth century. By the end of the nineteenth century 'dominion status' was being evolved, a convention whereby the same 'Crown' acted in accordance with the decisions of the British parliament in Britain, the Canadian parliament in Canada, and so on. But 'dominion status' came too late for the Channel Islands and was never applied there. The 'Crown' that acts in the islands is the British Crown, as advised by British ministers responsible to the British parliament at Westminster.

For formal and legal purposes it is with the Privy Council that the islands have to reckon. But Crown appointments come from the Home Office, and the Home Office exercises a general and nowadays an almost invariably beneficent surveillance over island affairs. Parliament also insists that it retains the power to legislate for the islands when it thinks fit, though latterly, except in matters of international concern, it has only done so with the acquiescence of the islands themselves but, were such a convention to be forgotten, what havoc in the domestic field might not a matter of international concern bring in its train.

This anomalous situation has naturally led to conflicts and misunderstandings from time to time, storms in teacups they may seem when looked back upon; but the issues were live enough at the time and many of them have implications still relevant to the present day. One such was the Case of the St Pancras Beadle. In 1831 the parish of St Pancras sent to Guernsey one of their beadles, Mr John Capes, with five paupers alleged to be chargeable for maintenance to parishes in the island. The Royal Court declared them to be not so chargeable, and Capes was required either to maintain or remove them. On his refusal he was himself detained in Guernsey for some months. St Pancras applied to the Lord Chief Justice of England for a writ of Habeas Corpus. The writ was duly served on the deputy sheriff of Guernsey, who paid no attention to it whatsoever. So the Lord Chief Justice sent one of his own tipstaffs with a warrant for the deputy sheriff's arrest. The only result was that the tipstaff on landing in Guernsey was brought before the Royal Court and himself taken into custody. The Royal Court knew, as the Lord Chief Justice had probably neglected to find out, two important facts: first, the specific one that the Act of Habeas Corpus had never applied in Guernsey; secondly, the more general one that none of the justices at Westminster had any authority to issue writs or to act in any other way in Guernsey.

Every charter granted to Guernsey or Jersey confirms and reiterates the basic liberty of the islanders to have cases tried in the islands and not carried outside except to the king himself in council. It would in the first place have been an intolerable burden for islanders to take cases, pleadings, witnesses and all overseas every time an appeal was made from the local courts; in addition—and more fundamental still—appeals would have meant taking cases from a court which knew and could apply the relevant law, Norman law, to a court which knew and used only the irrelevant English law. As for John Capes, in the end he was allowed to go back to St Pancras with his paupers, and Guernsey paid for their keep while they were in the island. The threatened extension of Habeas Corpus to the islands was dropped, and nothing more was heard of the Lord Chief Justice's writs and tipstaffs. A typical island compromise—small points conceded, the great principles confirmed.

Guernsey and Jersey

After the loss of Normandy the islands were at first governed by Wardens, appointed directly by the kings of England to represent them throughout the islands. The early wardens were responsible for the king's concern with defence, finance, and justice—but the administration of justice turned out to be no simple matter. As everywhere in the Middle Ages, the law observed was customary law; in Guernsey's case more or less the customary law of Normandy. Before 1204 Norman judges had visited the islands to hold assize, as they had everywhere in the duchy. After 1204 various expedients were tried; but eventually during the fourteenth century a pattern emerged which has had a profound effect on island history right down to the present day.

The law came to be administered in each of the major islands by a royal officer known as the king's bailiff, who was assisted—as is normal where customary law is in force—by a body of persons whose first duty was to declare the custom in each case. In the islands there were twelve of these jurats, and like the bailiff they had to be islanders so as to be familiar with local custom. Later this court, augmented by the notables of the islands, was to become the body which would petition the sovereign for changes in the law, and eventually it was to transform itself into a deliberative and legislative body as well. By the time the notables entitled to participate had been defined and fixed, the body became known as the States and took on a life more and more separate from that of the Royal Court from which it had sprung.

To this day, however, it is the Bailiff who presides over both court and States, and this has had important consequences because while the wardens were always charged with responsibility for the islands as a whole, bailiffs were from the start appointed separately for Jersey and Guernsey. So when the wardens' significance waned and that of the bailiffs and jurats waxed, the effective unit of administration became the island and remains very much so today.

Since the Middle Ages there have been practically no institutions common to the islands as a whole. Jersey and Guernsey each has its own bailiff, its own court, its own States; customary law has come to diverge a good deal over the centuries, and statute law naturally even more so. In addition, since the States have been active legislative bodies their actions have done much to shape the social and economic life of their islands, and this helps to explain the very different social and economic history and climate of Guernsey and Jersey.

Feudal beginnings

In the early part of the eleventh century, well before the conquest of England, Guernsey was granted by the dukes of Normandy in due feudal form to two of their greatest vassals, the Viscounts of Cotentin and Bessin, who each held about half of the island. No doubt each had on his lands, or fief, a court to dispense all justice except the very few suits reserved for the duke's own court. These lords would owe fealty to the duke for their lands and be required to pay him service or dues in respect of them, and no doubt in their turn they granted out the land to lesser men on similar terms.

The Middle Ages saw several processes at work which left their mark on the feudal system in Guernsey. The two great fiefs did not survive intact, many smaller ones taking their place; much land fell into the hands of ecclesiastics, usually monasteries; forfeitures were common, arising partly from the turbulence and rebellion appropriate to the period, but also more particularly from the separation from Normandy, which meant that those who hung on to their lands there lost those they held in Guernsey, and later that the monasteries holding Guernsey land, which were all French, were deprived of their fiefs as well—all this land reverted to the Crown; and, lastly, the formidable jurisdiction of the feudal lords was progressively restricted by the visits of ducal and royal assizes and by the eventual establishment of the Royal Court.

At the end of the Middle Ages, however, the fiefs were still active entities. Land could be held from a lord, or seigneur as he is termed in the islands in frank fief (as sub-fiefs in fact), as free tenements, or as villein land. The affairs of the fief were managed by a court, which would be convened at stated times by the seigneur. A court of Fief le Comte in 1406 is typical enough of the larger courts. It was presided over by the seneschal appointed by the seigneur, assisted by his greffier, or clerk. The 'jury' consisted of eight vavasseurs, who were in this case some of the tenants of the principal frank fiefs. The court's decisions were carried into effect by the prévôt and grangier. Certain tenants called bordiers, as duties due for their holdings, acted as police and officers of the court, which met at Courtil Beaucamp, or later at St George's Chapel and in a purpose-built courthouse. The court dealt with boundaries and matters of land ownership and took note of changes in tenancies as they occurred. These last were summarised once in a generation in a 'livre de perchage'—that is, a list, drawn up by a douzaine of tenants appointed by the seigneur and sworn by the court, of all the tenants of the fief with particulars of their holdings. The proceedings of the court concluded with a collation at the expense of the seigneur.

GUERNSEY

The court of the great fief St Michel (belonging to the Abbey of Mont-St-Michel) was responsible for a unique, originally trienniel, ceremony which survived till 1837—the Chevauchée de St Michel. This was apparently a kind of day-long island tour by the officers of the court, which seems to have incorporated several different layers of tradition. The officers of the Court of St Michel, accompanied by some of Guernsey's principal officers, perambulated the island on horseback, attended by about thirty pages on foot—handsome young men, known as the 'pions', whose privilege it was to kiss any woman they should meet on the route—and no doubt they met many. The chevauchée normally followed the same route, pausing to ride round certain stones as well as round the miller at the King's Mill; while at other stones the pions performed certain traditional dances. Collations were provided at fixed places, one at the west door of the Town Church being served by the king's sheriff and sergeant from a round table, which the chevauchée inevitably rode round too. One officer carried a wand 11ft 3in long and fined the owner of anything which obstructed the passage of that width. We can divine in the chevauchée traces of simple parish duties, of a concern for feudal precedence and boundaries, and no doubt memories of very ancient spring rites and the reverence due to the standing stones of ancient times.

Feudal survivals

How much of the feudal system survives in the Guernsey of today? The chevauchée was recently revived; but merely as a hollow charade on a summer's day.

The fiefs themselves certainly survive, though some of them are pitifully small, and to each fief its seigneur. For the tenants, all kinds of villein service have long since disappeared, as have champart, poulage, pesnage and moulage—rent paid in the form of corn or flax, fowls, pigs and flour—

134

on private fiefs. Property has been much sub-divided, and feudal dues with it. As late as 1887 the fief of Blanchelande was trying to collect dues amounting to 'one fowl, one half and one tenth of a fowl, one fortieth and one four-hundredth-and-eightieth of a fowl, twenty-eight eggs, three-quarters and one eighth of an egg'. History does not record if the egg was to be hard boiled.

Her Majesty's Receiver still collects some dues from the royal fiefs. Chefrente, which was a direct payment of money and in 1956 totalled less than £19, has not been collected since then. But a sum of 36p per household per annum in lieu of poulage is still collected from Fief le Roi, and 23½p per annum in lieu of quarantaine of eggs from Fief St Michel. The seigneur also had congé; and congé at least was worth having. Congé derived from the old treizième, and was long stabilised at one-thirteenth of the value of any real property sold on the fief. The proportion due to the seigneur was long calculated at 2 per cent. On the royal fiefs it brought the Crown well over £300,000 per annum, and could amount to thousands on the larger of the twenty private fiefs—so profitable was it in fact that its very profitability proved its undoing; the seigneurs' good fortune aroused envy in many an island breast, and congé was abolished (with some compensation) in 1976.

The livres de perchage and the seigneural courts are still kept up on some fiefs; the court of Fief Sausmarez, for instance, meets regularly every year. The livres are printed these days, but the high cost deters many courts. Ever since the seventeenth or eighteenth century the main business of the courts has been to note changes of tenancy on the fief, and any meetings held nowadays are almost exclusively formal. The court is convened at the traditional place, which may be, according to the fief, on a roadside, by a menhir, at the corner of a churchyard, in a manorial barn, or even—as at Sausmarez Manor—in a small courthouse built specially for the purpose. The seneschal presides, the vavasseurs report changes of tenancy since the last court, the greffier records the proceedings, and the business is over—except for one item: dinner at the seigneur's expense. Whatever feudal dues may lapse, that is one which never does.

The same tradition applies at the high feudal court of the island, the Queen's Court of Chief Pleas, where HM Receiver provides a dinner at the expense of Her Majesty at one of the three annual sittings which are held at Easter, at Michaelmas and in mid-January. This was originally the feudal court of the Crown, and was accordingly attended by the Crown's tenants-in-chief, just as the tenants of a seigneur attended his court. The seigneurs who are tenants-in-chief are still bound to attend the court either personally or by proxy of an advocate. It was therefore appropriately to a sitting of this court that the seigneurs of the island were summoned to pay homage and fealty, with due feudal pomp and ceremony, when Queen Elizabeth II visited Guernsey in 1957. The usual duties of the Queen's Court of Chief Pleas are a good deal less picturesque. It swears in special constables, and hears reports from the parishes on the cutting of brambles and hedges, the fencing of quarries, the management of watercourses, and other such mundane matters, though before the reforms of 1948 it had much more extensive powers. The court comprises—besides the seigneurs who for centuries now have merely answered their names when summoned and taken no further part in the proceedings—the bailiff and law officers and the twelve jurats. There also attend the constables of the ten parishes, who report on the matters with which the court deals.

These constables are not the village Bobbies. They are the principal officers of an ancient parish organisation still very much alive. In each parish the inhabitants elect the douzaine, a body of unpaid representatives still numbering twelve in most parishes, but sixteen in the Vale and twenty in St Peter Port, where it is the nearest thing to the Town Council. The douzaine choose from among themselves a senior and a junior constable, the senior of whom presides at their meetings, and a procureur of the poor, who dispenses relief to the needy of the parish and is a member of the parish poor-law committee. The douzaine is responsible for inspecting hedges and watercourses, for approving changes in alignment of fences, walls and buildings along highways, for keeping in repair parish pumps, drinking troughs and so on. They also report on applicants for licences, and assess the parish rate, or remède, which is authorised by the Royal Court. Nowadays it is becoming usual for the parish douzaine to be consulted or to give parish opinion on all kinds of public plans for changes in the parish; and this would seem to be a very sensible adaptation of an ancient institution to conditions as they are today.

THE LAW

The bailiff and jurats, constituting by themselves the Royal Court, have been central institutions in the island since the Middle Ages. In those days the king was the active fount of judicial, legislative and executive authority, and his officers tended to function as required in all three capacities. The bailiff and jurats were the managers of the king's affairs in the island, and they felt no need to distinguish between the various heads under which they operated. To this day the bailiff carries on this tradition. He is at the same time chief of the judicial, legislative, and executive arms of government. But nowadays the bailiff is almost a unique survival. Over the rest of the field of government the roles of judiciary, legislature, and executive are now as well separated as anywhere else—or at least as well as they are in Great Britain.

The bailiff and deputy-bailiff are still appointed by the sovereign by letters patent. The law officers—the Procureur de Sa Majesté and Comptroller de Sa Majesté, corresponding roughly to the attorney-general and solicitor-general—are appointed by royal commission. In addition the court is served by the Prévôt de Sa Majesté, or sheriff; the greffier, or clerk, and the serjeant.

The Royal Court

The Royal Court of Guernsey did not lose its legislative powers until 1948. Before that date the bailiff and jurats, sitting as the Court of Chief Pleas, had the power to issue what were called 'ordonnances', which were supposed to be 'regulations necessary for enforcing and putting into due execution the laws of the island', but which—especially before the turn of the century—often went far beyond that definition. The impropriety of this proceeding according to modern views was expressed by a commission as early as 1846: 'According to the theory of the Guernsey constitution, the jurats may on one day, sitting in a court of Chief Plaids, make an ordonnance without the consent of your majesty, against the will of the functionary representing the crown in the island, and without consulting the body of the States; and, on the next, sitting as a court of justice, may proceed to put their own construction on it and to execute the law of their own making, without their decision, in any matter of criminal law, being capable of review by any superior authority.'

The Royal Court nowadays confines itself to the administration of the law—the law of Guernsey, of course. It is not so different from English law, perhaps, as it once was. A good deal of British statute law has been freely adopted unaltered during the present century; a certain number of British Acts of Parliament have force in Guernsey by the explicit direction of Parliament; and, in fields where Guernsey customary law has provided no guidance, English precedents have increasingly been followed by the court. Nonetheless there is by now a considerable mass of Guernsey statute law —as much legislation was enacted in the three years 1956–58 as in the sixty-five years 1803–68—and Guernsey custom is still strong in the realm of real estate and inheritance.

Perhaps the most influential customary institutions have been partage and rentes, from which, taken together, the whole rural economy and landscape derive much of their character.

Partage

The custom of partage decreed the partition of the deceased's landed property between his direct heirs, according to rules which specified the proportions for sons and daughters, and the special right of the eldest son to the farm-house and immediate surroundings, the préciput. Such a system, if given free rein, is bound to have the effect of keeping estates small and in time probably reducing them to uneconomical dimensions. Young men trying to start up as farmers would find themselves possessed of insufficient land, and be compelled either to rent more and become largely tenant farmers or to borrow money to buy more, a solution open only to those able to offer security. Here the custom of rentes came to the rescue.

Rentes

A purchaser pays part of the price of a parcel of land in cash; the remainder of the price takes the form of rente— an obligation by the purchaser to pay a specified sum to the vendor each year. The critical point is that from the moment of the completion of the bargain the purchaser becomes the *owner* of the property and can only be dispossessed if he fails to pay the rente; thus the young farmer could start up with sufficient land of his own for the immediate outlay of only a small proportion of the purchase price, and often the eldest son could acquire the inheritance of brothers and sisters in this way, so preventing the break-up of the family farm. Rentes were originally paid in kind as wheat and were always expressed as quarters of wheat; the rente to be paid depended on the actual price of wheat at the time, which was declared each year at the Easter Chief Pleas. Since the 1920s the price of a quarter of wheat has been fixed and the value of rentes has declined with the value of money. The whole system resembles the system of emphyteusis in force in some parts of Europe, and it must have done much to render viable the mass of tiny properties which is the basis of Guernsey's rural economy.

Clameur de Haro

An undoubtedly Norman custom common to all the Channel Islands is the 'Clameur de Haro'. When an individual has reason to suppose himself wronged, but the ordinary process of law would be too slow to prevent the wrong, he falls on his knees at the spot where the wrong is alleged to be done, and in the presence of two witnesses calls out, 'Haro! Haro! Haro! A mon aide, mon prince! On me fait tort.' In Guernsey he must then repeat the Lord's Prayer in French, though in Jersey this is not thought necessary. The purpose of all this is the same as that of an injunction in England, to put an immediate stop to the disputed action until it can be brought to court and the rights and wrongs of the case thrashed out in the usual manner. The clameur is very much alive. Its use is continual but infrequent, just as it ought to be. It was raised against infringement of a neighbour's airspace by a crane in the Pollet in 1975. The crane's owners were fined as well for allowing the crane to swing over the property after the raising of the clameur.

THE STATES

While the Royal Court has now become an exclusively

judicial body, the legislative power in Guernsey has fallen into the hands of a comparative parvenu—the States of Deliberation. In fact there can be little doubt that the Royal Court and the States share a common origin; the States—at first a full or augmented meeting of the Court for special occasions —began to be distinguished from it in the sixteenth century and to assume a fixed form in the seventeenth, perhaps under the influence of the Calvinist synods and consistories of the period. The membership at that time was simple. The bailiff presided; the members were the twelve jurats, together with the rectors and senior constables of the ten parishes. We may suppose that the estates of the realm were here represented —the gentry by the jurats, the clergy by the rectors, and the people by the constables—though in the early days the whole body was recruited from the narrow top stratum of island society. At first the States met rarely and had little say in government. It was well into the last century before they were accepted as the representative assembly of the island. Since then their importance has increased and their representative character widened continuously. In 1841 Duncan could still refer to them in remarkably disparaging terms: 'There is no political institution more absurd, unjust, and defective than the administrative states of Guernsey.'

Almost immediately after that, in 1844, the constables of parishes were replaced by fifteen delegates from the douzaines, including six from previously under-represented St Peter Port. Directly elected deputies were added in 1899 and their number increased to eighteen in 1920, while about the same time the vote went to a much wider electorate. But it was after the experience of the German Occupation and at the prompting of the British government in 1948 that the most startling changes occurred.

Both the jurats and the rectors left the States of Deliberation for good, and the members now comprise, the bailiff as president; the procureur and comptroller as non-voting members; twelve conseillers, ten douzaine representatives, thirty-three directly elected people's deputies and two representatives from the States of Alderney. The conseillers are chosen by the States of Election, a separate body whose only business is the election of conseillers and jurats. It includes everybody who is anybody in political life—the bailiff, law officers and jurats, along with the conseillers, the deputies, twenty-four douzaine representatives and four from Alderney.

Politics in Guernsey do not run on party lines. There are no parties, no ins and outs in the States. The members sit according to their category and parish, and vote according to their personal view of the matters under discussion. Even the douzaine representatives, though they discuss coming States business with their douzaine, are not now bound to vote according to instructions from the douzaine, though they may well voice douzaine opinion in the debate. All this makes for refreshingly open and meaningful discussion. A deputy may rise, as I have heard one do, and announce: 'I came to the States firmly intending to support this motion. I have listened to the debate, and I now propose to oppose it.' When were such words last to be heard at Westminster?

The island's administrative business is organised rather on the same lines as that of an English county or district. The States members are elected to committees each of which takes charge of one branch of the administration and answers for it to the States. The administrative officers are responsible for carrying out the policies of the committee—so long as they enjoy the support of the States—and head a civil service as devoted to duty and as prone to proliferation as any on the mainland.

HM REPRESENTATIVE

The bailiff represented the Crown in the Royal Court, which grew into the States, and to this day when the lieutenant-

Page 143 Occasions: *(above)* inauguration of the lieutenant-governor, Sir Charles Mills being sworn in by the Bailiff in the Royal Court in 1969; *(below)* the Chevauchée being re-enacted on a summer day, the squires or pions picnicking by tradition round the Table des Pions at Pleinmont

Page 144 (above) Herm is only a mile and a half long, but a great deal of variety is packed into this miniature island *(Aerofilms)*; *(below)* away from it all at Petit Port Bay

governor attends the States, which he often does, he occupies
a chair at a lower level than the bailiff's. He is treated with
great respect there, but he may not vote, and speaks only
on those occasions when he must do so as Her Majesty's
representative.

The duties of the lieutenant-governor are nowadays, except
for his immigration and passport office, almost entirely
ceremonial. His role is similar to that of the governor-general
of a Commonwealth country, who represents locally the
absent constitutional monarch; though there is a distinction
in that the Guernsey government takes no formal part in his
appointment, which is made by the Home Office as adviser
to the sovereign. But lieutenant-governors were not always
thus. They were originally appointed as representatives of
absent governors, and enjoyed considerable power, especially
in time of war or rumours of war.

The post of governor was abolished in 1835. Governors
had rarely visited Guernsey except in time of war or threat
of war. Many of them looked upon the appointment mainly
as a source of revenue, if not a sinecure, though several
showed genuine interest in the island and, being men of
power and position, could often give valuable help in high
places. Their supersession brought the island nearer to the
Crown by introducing in the new-style lieutenant-governor
a direct representative of majesty instead of a subject's
nominee.

Until World War II, lieutenant-governors commanded
the garrison, and perhaps would again if there was one. This
gave them more leverage than they enjoy today, and deference
to the officer class from which they came helped to give them
standing and a chance to intervene substantially in island
affairs; though they needed to behave with tact and discretion,
as the famous but peppery Lieutenant-General Napier
discovered in the last century. He fell foul of the bailiff,
jurats and people so often through his high-handed actions

I

that London came to doubt the loyalty of Guernsey and at one stage sent over an 'expeditionary force' of 600 men supposedly to ensure the security of the lieutenant-governor. It has even been suggested that Queen Victoria's visit of 1846, the first by a reigning sovereign of England, was made largely to mollify the islanders after these absurdities.

SYMBOLS AND SERVICES

The arms

FEW visitors to the island can fail to become aware of its most prominent symbol of authority in the island, the shield of red with three golden leopards prancing defiantly across it, surmounted by what looks like a little sprig of some rather meagre and perhaps xerophilous plant. The three leopards will be quite familiar to visitors from Britain; they occur in the royal arms and on the royal standard of the United Kingdom, but there quartered with the single rampant lion of Scotland and the harp of Ireland. The three leopards are the English leopards, carried alone on the shield of the royal house of England from the time when arms were first distinguished until Edward III claimed the throne of France and quartered the French lilies with them. Some time after the loss of Normandy it became obvious that the king's bailiffs in the Channel Islands needed a seal to enable them to transact their business adequately. Edward I accordingly sent a seal of his own to the islands—'quoddam sigillum nostrum . . . fecimus provideri'—and, of course, Edward's seal bore Edward's arms. A few years later it was found to be inconvenient to dispose of only one seal for all the islands, and the king sent separate ones to Jersey and Guernsey. Guernsey's happened to have a little embellish-

147

ment at the top, which may have been just a *jeu d'esprit* of the seal-maker or may have been intended as a stop to the inscription 'S' Ballivie Insule de Gernereye' (Seal of the Bailiff of the Island of Guernsey) which surrounded the shield. Jersey's seal had no such sprig; and the distinction between Jersey's plain shield and Guernsey's sprigged shield has been jealously maintained ever since. 'Guernsey's shield' one can say because, although it is obviously none other than the king of England's, over the centuries it has become accepted as the emblem of Guernsey, and its use as such was approved by King Edward VII in 1905, when His Majesty was 'graciously pleased to sanction the continued use of the Arms as at present claimed'.

The flag

During King Edward VII's reign Guernsey became the approved possessor of a flag as well, but this time rather by virtue of a bureaucratic blunder. In 1906 a copy of a letter from the Home Office approving the arms in accordance with His Majesty's wishes was forwarded to the Royal Court from the lieutenant-governor's office with the word 'flag' replacing the word 'arms' and was so entered in the Livre d'Ordonnances, thus acquiring the force of law. Guernsey people had, probably only a little before that time, begun to use St George's flag as their own, and this is certainly the one which was presumed to have been approved by the ordonnance and which can be seen flying over the States Offices and in other public places on land today. But on land only—St George's flag when flown at sea at the main signifies the presence on board of a full admiral, and its use in any other circumstances is sternly forbidden on pain of frightful penalties by the Merchant Shipping Act of 1894. The flag of Guernsey has nonetheless seen service afloat. When the *White Heather* ran between Guernsey and Sark during the Occupation, the use of the red ensign would clearly have been unacceptable to the Germans; so, in order to avoid flying the hated swastika, the flag of Guernsey was flown instead. It may also be true that a bailiff of the years between the wars once visited HMS *Nelson* flying St George's flag on his pinnace. The ship's company was fallen in, the 'admiral' was piped aboard, the officer of the watch asked his name and standing. The story does not record in detail the captain's reaction when informed that he had laid on full naval honours for 'a bailiff'.

The flower

Up to 4,000ft on the slopes of Table Mountain in South Africa there grows wild a marvellous lily with pink or crimson flowers suffused with a radiance like golden dew— the national flower of Guernsey, *Nerine sarniensis*, the Guernsey lily. How did a wild flower from the Cape of Good Hope come to be linked, even in scientific terminology, with a small island in the English Channel?

The best-known and most romantic story attributes the plant to the shipwreck on the Guernsey coast, soon after the Restoration, of a Dutch merchantman on passage from Japan—where it was long supposed, the lily originated. The bulbs were washed on to the dunes and flowered spontaneously a few years later.

The lily is known to have been grown by Morin in Paris as early as 1634 and was in cultivation in England by 1659 in the Wimbledon garden of Sir John Lambert, successful Parliamentary general and ardent horticulturist. Sir John was sent as a prisoner to Castle Cornet after the Restoration and remained in Guernsey ten years. A possible inference is that he introduced the lily to the island during his far from rigorous confinement there.

For a description of the lily we can scarcely do better than quote from Hoffman's hyperbolical broadsheet of 1729:

So this fair Lilly does revive,
And each seventh year, spring, bloom and thrive,
Whose Scent more Sweetness does disclose,
Than Clove and Pink, and Damask Rose,
Whose Scents and Colours join'd in one,
Are by this Lilly fair, out-done;

Whose Lilly-bud divides in three,
To give ten Stalks their Liberty;
A six-leaf'd Flow'r from each Stalk streams,
From each Flow'r flow seven radiant Beams,
Which from seven well-set Rubies stream,
And makes each Flow'r a Diadem:
All which in Blush and Bloom unfold
Aurora decked in Dew of Gold.

CURRENCY

Guernsey currency has a long and chequered history. When the separation from Normandy took place in the thirteenth century there was no corresponding change of currency. Livres of Tours, divided into twenty sols of twelve deniers each, continued in use; and feudal dues, including the king's, continued to be paid and reckoned in this way. Unfortunately for the seigneurs, the French currency almost immediately started to lose value as against the English, and there were already serious arguments in the fourteenth century about the currency to be used for paying the royal taxes. The islanders won of course, and continued to pay in depreciated tournois. It was lucky for them that they did, because by the time of the French Revolution the livre tournois had depreciated to one seventy-eighth of its nominal value in gold. In Guernsey things never quite came to this pass because the value of £1 tournois was fixed in Queen Anne's reign at one fourteenth of £1 sterling. The livre tournois ceased to be anything but a money of account in 1829 when the French currency was put on a solid footing with the introduction of the franc. One franc was divided in Guernsey into ten pence 'currency' and did service for nearly a century.

British currency made its way more and more in the island, being admitted to equal legal status with the franc in 1870, and a curious relationship resulted which never failed to call for comment by visitors: 240 Guernsey pence were equal to £1 Guernsey, or 'currency'; ten Guernsey pence being equal to one franc, 240 Guernsey pence equalled 24 francs, which for many years had the value of just over 19s sterling, the sum usually being made up by allowing, for £1 currency, 19s sterling plus 2½d currency. It can be imagined that holders of sterling had to have their wits about them to avoid paying in sterling for goods quoted in currency; and, even when the difference was allowed for, the calculations were usually beyond the comprehension of any but islanders. All this was swept away in 1921, when sterling became the only legal currency and about ten tons of French silver were withdrawn from circulation.

Currency notes were first issued by the States in 1816, and there were several other issues in the early nineteenth century. These issues were at first made only for specific purposes—the Doyle monuments and the New Markets being the best known—and were redeemed within a few years. With the shortage of currency during World War I, States paper money became an established institution, and the management of the currency shows a useful little profit to the treasury. There has recently been over £3·5 million of States currency in circulation.

Guernsey claims to have always had the right of coinage; in fact the earliest clearly authenticated official issue of coins was undertaken ostensibly 'in order to preserve the ancient privilege of the island'. This was in 1623 when ferlukes, which had the value of half a denier, were ordered to be struck. Regular issues of doubles in values of one to eight were made from 1830 on; at first in copper, after 1864 in bronze. The double or liard began to be used in the eighteenth century, when there were six or seven to the livre tournois. It was later reckoned as an eighth of a penny, currency or sterling, according to period.

From 1956 on a more active coinage policy was initiated. Attractive new designs showing the Guernsey lily replaced the drab Victorian eight and four double pieces, and were accompanied by a bizarre threepenny bit adorned with a handsome Guernsey cow and distinguished by a unique wavy edge. This was followed in 1966 by an even more bizarre 'square' coin—with rounded corners, however—which was struck to the value of 10s to commemorate the Norman conquest of England and showed appropriately the head of the conquering duke himself. The profits accruing to the States' coffers from these issues, especially the last, recommended coinage to all good Guernseymen, and decimalisation was the occasion for a full set of Guernsey coins conveniently corresponding in size and denomination with those of the United Kingdom. In accordance with a tradition broken only for the 'Norman Conquest 10s' the sovereign's head does not appear on these coins, each bearing on the obverse the seal of the bailiwick instead. On the reverse the 1p shows an Alderney gannet, the 2p Sark mill, the 5p a Guernsey lily, the 10p a Guernsey cow, and the 50p a cap of maintenance, which is thought to have been, in English medieval usage, the prerogative of dukes and was worn till 1801 by the gentlemen who represented at coronations the Dukes of Normandy and Aquitaine.

POSTAL SERVICES

It might have been supposed that Guernsey would have issued its own postage stamps from the beginning as the British colonies did. But the Guernsey posts were in the hands of the General Post Office well before the first postage stamps were dreamed of. Parliament passed in 1794 an Act for extending the powers of the GPO to the Channel Islands, and it was registered in the same year by the Royal Court in Guernsey, which thus surrendered for 175 years the island's chance of controlling its own posts. The Guernsey post office grew and prospered in an an orderly and uneventful manner as a simple branch of the GPO for the next 146 years—that is, until the fateful day in June 1940 when the island fell under German occupation. From then on Guernsey was on its own.

By October 1940 stamps were beginning to run short. New stamps were prepared but took some time to receive German approval. In the meantime 1d stamps ran right out, and permission was given by post office notice of 24 December 1940 for the use of 2d stamps cut in half. The new stamps themselves were designed austerely by E. W. Vaudin to show simply the Arms of Guernsey (without sprig!) and the words 'Guernsey' above and 'Postage' below, with the value. They were typographed at the 'Guernsey Press', $\frac{1}{2}$d and 1d values coming out in early 1941. The 2$\frac{1}{2}$d value had to wait till 1944; it went like hot cakes, 80,000 being sold on the first day alone. Over the whole four years of Occupation nearly 5 million Guernsey stamps were printed, though it is doubtful if postal use accounted for much more than half of them. Production was beset with difficulties; many of the sheets were gummed by brushing on by hand a mixture of gum, dextrine and any other adhesives that happened to be available. In March 1942 a watermarked French paper was used for a while. It absorbed the gum, which turned it blue, and provided a field day for collectors. The stamps were sold out in three weeks. In the very difficult days of blockade at the end of the war the stock of stamps was completely exhausted and, from March 1945 on, hand cancellations reading simply 'PAID' were used instead of stamps.

After the war the Guernsey posts reverted to the control of the GPO; two series of stamps were, however, issued for use in the island, though these remained British stamps and were good anywhere in the UK as well as in Guernsey. The first was a rather sad little issue in 1948 of two stamps showing carts collecting vraic and intended to commemorate the liberation of the Channel Islands. The second was part of Dr Hill's quaint and constitutionally absurd series of 'regional' stamps, which provided, along with special designs for Jersey, Guernsey and the Isle of Man, equivalent issues for perfectly normal parts of the United Kingdom like Wales and Scotland, but nothing for England, which the doctor seemed not to have heard of. Guernsey's design was by E. A. Piprell, and featured a Guernsey lily and a crown taken from a Norman silver penny of William I. These were in use from 1958 on.

The most important event since 1794 in the postal history of Guernsey occurred in 1969. In that year the GPO ceased to be a service administered under the prerogative and was assimilated to the pattern of the nationalised public utilities. None of these operated in the Channel Islands for sound constitutional reasons; and the British government accordingly offered the islands the opportunity of taking charge of their own posts. Jersey and Guernsey made a quick calculation, and accepted gladly. Administrative machinery was put in motion, and on 1 October 1969 the Guernsey Post Office was born. The birth was celebrated with a dignified set of sixteen stamps and Guernsey launched itself into philately with a howler. The 1d and 1s 6d stamps showed a map of the bailiwick—but the bailiwick seemed to be located in rough country about 75 miles east of Madrid in latitude 40° 30′ N longitude 2° 30′ W; someone along the line had copied a latitude of 49° 30′ as 40° 30′ and no one noticed until it was too late. Since then production has been more careful and an average of three faultless and attractive, though sometimes suspiciously aimless, issues has been made each year.

TELEPHONE SYSTEM

The island's telephone system was established in 1896–7, following a successful campaign to rout the National Telephone Company. This company had obtained a Post Office licence, as was the manner of working in those days, to set up telephone systems in the United Kingdom. The States had already applied for a Post Office licence to operate telephones in Guernsey; but the company was determined nevertheless to extend its activities to the island and in spite of its licence being confined to the UK. It applied to the constables of St Peter Port for permission to put up wires for two subscribers in the town, and this was granted. Very early on the morning of 1 June 1896 the company erected a pole behind the Central Schools and extended wires from it in all directions. The constables and the States were faced with a fait accompli. But they were quite equal to the situation; on the morning of 3 June the constables cut all the company's wires down again. Owing to the astuteness of the constables in taking action themselves, it was the company which was compelled to go to law, claiming damages from the constables. It fought the case right through to the Privy Council and lost. The way was now open for the States and, in spite of a certain amount of underhand play by the Post Office and the National Telephone Company (which need not detain us here), they obtained their licence in 1897 and have administered the island telephone system ever since. External telecommunications were transferred from the Post Office to the States in 1973.

PUBLIC UTILITIES

In an island of Guernsey's size, population and sophistication there are many public services which present no problems more serious than are encountered in places of a similar scale on the mainland. The island administers its own police, fire service, sewage, hospitals, prisons and schools. In some cases expert advice is called upon from the United Kingdom; and, for example, long-term and special prisoners are regularly sent there by arrangement.

Gas used to be made at Longstore, but it is now imported and only treated in the island. Electricity is still generated at St Sampson's; there is no question of putting Guernsey on the grid, and this may make for marginally higher costs in the long run; but that is all.

Refuse disposal may lead to special difficulties on a crowded island. But Guernsey has been lucky; the abandoned quarries of the northern parishes provide ready-made rubbish tips which are calculated to suffice for many years to come. Then the island will have a real headache; but till then it is only the neighbours of the pits who can complain of the nuisance, and luckily no pit is bottomless and no single pit needs to be any sort of nuisance for ever.

Water supply

The question of water supplies gives some cause for concern. The island receives in an average year 12,500 million gallons of water from the heavens; and if this could all be caught it would satisfy the present demand ten times over. But, of course, it cannot all be caught; nor does it fall so plentifully every year. The present demand of 1,250 million gallons a year, rising by about 30 million gallons annually, seems high on an island almost without industry. But glasshouses are voracious of water, and something like half of Guernsey's consumption goes into them.

The great bulk of the water used is taken from surface runoff. Some 7 or 8 per cent comes from five wells in the upper parishes. The remainder is abstracted from some of the principal streams or flows direct into the reservoir. Between them these surface sources tap a catchment of 11·2sq miles, almost half the island. Storage is provided for 720 million gallons, to allow for the use in summer of winter excess. The quarries come in useful here again, accounting for two-thirds of the total. The remainder is stored in the fine reservoir completed in 1947 which occupies three small valleys at St Saviour's. There are three stations for treatment, though many growers receive water raw for their green-houses. The treated water is stored in a 5 million-gallon covered reservoir on the Forest Road; this must have become a landmark for many a visitor coming in to town from the airport, as it is bounded by an exceptionally fine belt of conifers which relieves that rather undistinguished drive.

Guernsey seems to manage for water well enough. Nevertheless the supply of an island, where the area and the precipitation to be tapped are inexorably limited, is always precarious. At the end of the very difficult 1971 season the day was saved only by the public spirit of the people, who in October cut consumption by voluntary savings from a usual 3 million to 2 million gallons a day.

An attempt to adapt sea water to supplement the island's supply proved unsatisfactory. A desalination plant set up in 1960 lacked sufficient capacity and was costly to run. It was finally abandoned in favour of expansion by more conventional means.

HERM

'A goose,' said Dr Johnson, 'is a silly bird, too much for one and not enough for two.' I hesitate to call Herm 'silly', but it is still an awkward size like the goose— too big to be treated just as an offshore part of Guernsey, but scarcely big enough (it is less than a square mile in area) to stand on its own like Sark or Alderney. Progress in Herm has always seemed to be initiated by impulse from outside, and when that impulse has slackened or failed the island has fallen back into passivity or worse. It is a very long time since there was to be found on Herm a self-supporting and self-reproducing community such as Sark has nourished since the seventeenth century and Alderney since the dawn of history.

All the Channel Islands tend to have specialised existences, and not only specialised existences but sudden and far-reaching changes as well. It is probably a result of the narrowness and precariousness of the island base. If this holds true for a 'big' island like Guernsey, it is likely to hold even truer for little Herm; so it is not at all surprising to find the tiny island harbouring at different times a succession of quite different and usually highly specialised ways of life.

History
Herm has been a seat of piety, of industry, of pleasure, and

of profit. Piety is the first we have evidence for. In prehistoric times some have believed it was used as a burial ground for the dead of Guernsey, so numerous seemed the remains of interments on so small a compass. When the islands were converted to Christianity, Herm served first perhaps as a hermitage, then more certainly for a monastery, which was colonised from Cherbourg and survived until the Reformation swept it away. Since that time profit and pleasure have disputed the scene.

The most valuable economic resource of Herm has been the rock of which it is made. At the time when Guernsey granite was in its heyday, Herm was not overlooked. The works were from first to last in the hands successively of the tenant of the time, Lt Col Lindsay, and of John Duncan, a Guernsey historian who later married Lindsay's illegitimate daughter. Between them they worked quarries on Herm for about twenty years, starting in 1824. At the height of the boom about 1840 there were said to be 400 people on the island. Some of them were Aberdonian craftsmen, but most were pretty rough Irish labourers, many living in cabins knocked up from driftwood and turf, and subsisting largely on gin, duty unpaid. There were also substantial buildings at the quay, a brewery and at one time a school for forty children, also an extensive harbour capable of handling 600 tons of stone in a day. All this activity ended rather suddenly in bankruptcy, as did the contemporary attempt to mine copper, lead and silver near Rosière landing.

Tenants

For much of the seventeenth and eighteenth centuries Herm lay more or less deserted, serving mostly as a rabbit warren and game preserve, and understood to be at the disposal of the lieutenant-governor. After 1737 it was let by the Crown to a succession of gentlemen, most of whom, after the quarrying era, looked upon it as a romantic retreat from the world; to them we still owe a great deal of the present landscape. Belvoir House was built there by Col Feilden (tenancy commencing 1867); the White House can only be said to have grown itself, while the Manor took its present incongruous and uncompromising shape under Prince Blücher von Wahlstatt (1889–), though he made up for it by laying out the manor garden. Compton Mackenzie (1920–) describes the one as 'externally as ugly a building as may be seen in Europe' and the other as 'intersected by broad ilex-bordered walks that are worthy of the Borghese Gardens'. The prince also planted many of the trees that are now in their maturity—including the blue gums 'the rattle of whose leaves in the wind is like a bunch or rusty keys in the hand of a caretakers' (Compton Mackenzie again of course); though the vast, sombre and exciting Monterey pines and cypresses were left by—of all people—the Trappists, who leased Herm for a short period in 1882.

Most of these tenants took Herm as a pleasure retreat and drew the money they spent on it from sources far away. The present tenant, Major Peter Wood, has always looked at life from a very different angle. He and his family have identified themselves absolutely with the island. They live there and have no other home; they have striven for over twenty years to make Herm a going concern, a source of livelihood rather than a plaything. In addition to the tenant's own family there is now a permanent Herm population of about a dozen families, augmented every summer very considerably by those who come to work in the seasonal trades. In many ways life is less exotic than it was in the old days; but there are still problems to face when one lives on such a small island.

Economy

The Herm farm is reputed the biggest in the Channel Islands, all 100 acres of it. It is now a dairy farm, though the Woods at one time tried turning some of it over to daffodils

160

for the English market, and the last tenant, A. G. Jefferies, who worked hard to rehabilitate Herm after the German occupation, unaccountably stocked it with forty donkeys—whatever would one want with forty donkeys on Herm? The dairy herd now numbers near 150—all Guernseys, of course—and produces about 160 gallons of milk a day, which suffices amply for the summer population and gives rise to a daily export to Guernsey in winter. Apart from the farm practically the whole economy revolves round the visitors. The White House Hotel, founded by Col Feilden in the 1870s, has been greatly enlarged, and can put up about ninety visitors at a time in comfort; but the really big business is with day trippers. Every visitor to Guernsey must feel an urge to make the trip to the little island so temptingly displayed in full view of St Peter Port—and most of them do. Trippers run to around 100,000 in a year, and can number 2,000 in a single day. Guernsey boats bring them across; but once they set foot on Herm the tenant takes over. There is a pub, a restaurant, a tea-house by the beach, and shops in an attractive and unexpected Italian-style and Italian-built piazza—not to mention a landing fee, much of which is earmarked for public works.

Services

There is a regular school for about a dozen pupils with a full-time teacher. Electricity is generated on the island. The tenant, after suffering very badly from drought in his very first year, has laid a ring water main fed from springs, and has more recently installed an efficient sewage system. Telephone communications are maintained by a radio-telephone link with Guernsey, and Herm claims the smallest fully automated public telephone exchange in the world. The posts have been a more knotty problem. Jefferies for a time ran a pigeon post between Herm and St Peter Port. This was more exotic than practical; but the private postal service to Guernsey, which he started in face of a GPO refusal to operate, proved a great success. The reason was that the tenant charged for this carriage by means of stamps, which (though classed as 'locals' by serious collectors) caught the imagination of the public and brought in a steady profit even when no letters were carried. Unfortunately for Herm, Guernsey went in for the philatelic business itself when it took over the post office, and the States suppressed all competition within the bailiwick. Now there is a simple sub-post office in Herm, just like that in any Guernsey village —except that the tenant is inevitably himself the sub-post-master. He is the parson too, in a manner of speaking, being the one who normally holds service on Sundays in the strong and charming little chapel of St Tugual which lies right alongside the Manor House. But he is neither physician nor policeman, both of these being called over from Guernsey when they are needed, sometimes in dramatic circumstances —on one occasion even Guernsey's regular 'marine ambulance' found the going too severe, and the lifeboat had to be called out to get the doctor across.

Landscape

All this history and activity is rather improbably packed into a space only 1½ miles long by ½ mile wide. The main block of the island, which carries the farm, is a plateau like a slightly lower miniature of the Guernsey plateau, with the same undulating surface and steep-sloped edges, which give rise to delightfully varied and interesting coastline, sometimes dropping abruptly into deep, clear water, sometimes opening to little bays or to frighteningly sudden narrow indentations. The plateau top constitutes the farmland, divided by stone walls into big fields and bisected by a straight narrow lane running north and south the whole of its length. It also carries the farm buildings and the farm workers' houses, as well as the manor house, chapel and gardens, and the home of the present tenant. Almost everyone else in the community lives near the landing pier, on a narrow level between the plateau slope and the shore. The tide here dries so far that at low water boats are forced to come in to the rude steps at Rosière, which lies 400yd to the southward along a delicious blackthorn-bordered lane. The steep coast beyond the steps carries mainly furze, bramble, bracken and coarse grass, and can be circumambulated comfortably by the active visitor.

All that takes up the southern three-quarters of the island; but for most people the principal attraction lies in the north. Here is no plateau, but a low, square, sandy plain with a brackish lake in the middle and the sea on three sides, and on each side dunes bordering a first-class beach. The most famous and popular of these beaches is on the east side; it is named the Shell Beach and is built of a multitude of broken and entire shells which by their variety, beauty and strangeness can help to fill a lazy summer's day with delight and wonder.

JETHOU

Only $\frac{1}{4}$ mile to the south-west of Herm lies an even smaller island, Herm's satellite, Jethou. Jethou is only $\frac{1}{2}$ mile long and covers about 40 acres; but it repeats the same basic form as its bigger neighbours. It has the same steep-sloped rim, capped by the same plateau top—but here the plateau is only big enough for two or three tiny fields, and the impression from a distance is less of a dignified whale or a surfaced submarine than of a pork-pie hat thrown nonchalantly on the water.

The glory of Jethou is in the spring, when the wild flowers surpass anything to be seen on the other islands. The little wood now known sadly as the Fairy Wood is the finest sight of all and has more than spring flowers to recommend it. 'On the East side,' writes Compton Mackenzie, 'was a little wood of gnarled and stunted trees, their trunks and branches covered with thick lichen, presumably to protect themselves against the fierce gales which swept across from Sark ... I have seen nowhere so thick a carpet of bluebells when their chimes were ringing summer in, and in spring along the edge of that little wood were many hoop-petticoat daffodils . . . That little wood marked the boundary for primroses. Beyond it not one showed itself. The slopes south-east and south were covered instead with sea-pinks and white campion, with here and there the sombre green of butcher's broom in which one or two of the island's wrens used to nest.'

From Jethou's landing place the Manor House lies a short walk to the westward. A house is known to have been here since at least 1710; but the present one is a conversion of outhouses and stables dating from the early part of the last century. The garden boasts a magnificent ancient mulberry tree still in full production; but it is not as a whole cultivated to the level of the 1930s when Compton Mackenzie sent to Tresco for many wonderful echiums. Most of these have disappeared, though one which quite likely derives from this batch is to be found flaunting its annual 10ft of grey-blue flower in many a Channel Island garden to this day. There is also a well 36ft deep, full of water in winter but dry in summer; at the bottom is a small chamber 3ft wide, 5ft long and 4ft high cut in the well's side from the solid rock—a smuggler's hideaway as likely as not, and an ingenious one at that.

Jethou first enters history in the eleventh century, when it was granted by Duke Robert the Devil as a reward for a conspicuous service at sea to one Restauld, who later transferred it to the monastery of Mont St Michel. By the eighteenth century the Crown was letting Jethou to tenants, whose names are known from 1717. Several of them were noted smugglers; the most daring tenant of recent years being Col Widdicombe, whose home was raided by the

Guernsey police in 1954 because he was serving drinks on a Sunday. The most famous tenant of this century, however, was Compton Mackenzie, who migrated from Herm in 1923 and stayed on till 1934.

The last tenant, Andrew Faed, established a small community on Jethou rather in the manner of Major Wood on Herm. He and his family lived on the island, with a man and wife to help, plus up to three or four extra in the season. He ran the island for visitors in the summer, keeping a shop and café and even a restaurant. For some years he farmed about 4 vergees of ploughed land, growing potatoes and broccoli, with some roots for two cows which mostly grazed free. Daffodils planted by the previous tenant were picked and marketed too.

The present tenant, Sir Charles Hayward, uses Jethou as his private home and retreat. The farm has been given up; the daffodils are not picked; the only domestic animals are a few fowl kept for household purposes. There are no trips for visitors. The population averages eight or nine, and consists exclusively of the tenant with his family and staff.

Appendix

GUERNSEY'S NORTH-AMERICAN CONNECTIONS

Guernsey County, Ohio, is a true daughter of Guernsey. T. E.
Williams gives an account of its progress in a book published in
Cleveland in 1882 entitled *The Household Guide and Instructor,
with Biographies of the Presidents of the United States and a
brief outline of the History of Guernsey County, Ohio.*

In 1806 the brothers Thomas, Nicholas, John and Peter
Sarchet, with Daniel Ferbrache their brother-in-law, emigrated
from Guernsey to the New World. Their adventures began even
before they reached Jersey, for on the crossing two men were
pressed from their craft for the navy, whereupon Thomas Sarchet
on landing in Jersey went straight to 'the Governor' (more likely
the bailiff) and laid information which enabled the Court to
secure their release, the navy having no right to press islanders.
Thomas Sarchet was not the kind of man to look on while wrong
was done—had not his own grandfather fled from France as a
stripling rather than submit to his parents' refusal to allow him
to read his bible? Now our Thomas was a licensed Methodist
Episcopal exhorter.

The small Guernsey party endured the long crossing to
Norfolk, Virginia, and at length set out from Baltimore in
waggons and on foot for Cincinnati. After thirty days on the trail
they rested their horses near Wheeling; but the beasts quickly
became so fat they were useless. The party hired a new train
and with much trouble reached Cambridge, Ohio, on the day of
a sale of lots. Fed up with travelling, they bought eleven lots and
settled down there, building a cabin to last out the winter. Next

166

spring they were joined by James Bichard, William Ogier, Thomas Naftel, Thomas Lenfestey, Daniel Hubert, Peter Corbet, John Robin, Peter and John Torade, and Nicolas Podwin (*sic*). The Sarchets became leaders of the community, opening the first shop, building the first brick house, and holding there the first religious meetings where Thomas Sarchet and William Ogier, a preacher of the Methodist Episcopal Church, officiated. We can see that these men were true Guernseymen of their time by the description we have of them: 'Although the settlers here were generally of a religious nature, and drunkenness and quarrels almost unknown, yet many believed in witchcraft and some professed to be witchdoctors with the power to counteract the influence of evil spirits.'

In 1810 the State of Ohio created a new county round Cambridge and named it Guernsey in honour of the Guernsey settlers. There are said still to be Guernsey names in that part of Ohio.

Guernsey, Iowa was laid out in 1884. A large number of settlers were Ohio people and many of them came from Guernsey County of that state. From the old home county they selected the name Guernsey for the town. The habit of carrying names on to new settlements was a common and natural one in America, and many a name crossed the Atlantic only to be carried westward again one, two, or even three times, and names originating on the eastern seaboard or in the early western regions were subject to the same general tendency.

Guernsey, Wyoming was named after the ranch owner, Mr Guernsey, and has no known connection with the island.

Sarnia, Ontario was known as The Rapids until 1835 when the hundred or so inhabitants grew tired of this name but could not agree on a better one. Sir John Colborne, who was then governor of Upper Canada and had just served four years as lieutenant-governor of Guernsey, happened to visit the village and suggested the name Sarnia. Sir John was a veteran of the Peninsula and of Waterloo. When lieutenant-governor he had been largely responsible for the rehabilitation of Elizabeth College. He retired from the army and was appointed field-marshal at the age of eighty-two.

Guernsey, Saskatchewan is a tiny (pop 206) prairie town incorporated in 1907. The origin of the name seems to be unknown, but there seems little doubt it derives from Guernsey because of the street names: St George's Street, St Martin's Street, St Peter's Street, St Sampson's Street, Dixcart Street, Cobo Avenue and Hanois Avenue—which must be about as many streets as are needed for 206 people.

BIBLIOGRAPHY

Two sources are indispensable to any study of Guernsey. One is the *Reports and Transactions of the Société Guernesiaise*, published annually since 1882, up till 1926 as *Reports and Transactions of the Guernsey Society for Natural Science and Local Research*. The other is the publications of the Island's government. These include the Population Census; Reports and Censuses from States committees, Agriculture, Horticulture, Fishing, Tourism, etc; and the *Billets d'Etat*, agenda for meetings of the States, which often carry reports on or summaries of topics coming under discussion.

ANSTED, D. T. and LATHAM, R. *The Channel Islands* (London, 1862)

BAKER, E. J. *Stamps of the Channel Islands* (Guernsey, 1949)

BENNETT, A. R. *History of the States of Guernsey Telephone System 1895–1925* (London, 1926)

BONAMY, S. *Account of Guernsey* (MS, 1749)

BONSOR, N. P. *The Guernsey Railway* (Lingfield, 1967)

BRANTHWAITE, J. and MACLEAN, F. *Two Knapsacks in the Channel Islands* (London, 1896)

CAREY, E. F. *Essays on Guernsey History* (Guernsey, 1936)

——. *The Channel Islands* (London, 1940)

Catholicism in the Channel Islands, a Symposium (Guernsey, 1951)

CLIFF, W. H. *History, Flora, Fauna, and Guide to the Island of Jethou in the Channel Islands* (Guernsey, 1960)

COLLENETTE, V. G. *Elizabeth College 1563–1963* (Guernsey, 1963)

COURTVRIEND, V. V. *Isolated Island* (Guernsey, 1949)

BIBLIOGRAPHY

COYSH, V. 'History of Aviation in the Guernsey Bailiwick', *Guernsey Star* (4 May 1964)

CRUICKSHANK, C. *The German Occupation of the Channel Islands* (Oxford, 1975)

DE GARIS, M. (ed). *An English–Guernsey Dictionary* (Guernsey, 1967)

DE GUÉRIN, B. C. *The Norman Isles* (Hadleigh, 1948)

DELANY, M. J. and HEALY, M. J. R. 'Variation in the Long-tailed Field-mouse in the Channel Islands', *Proceedings of the Royal Society of Botany*, vol 166, p408 (1967)

——. 'Variation in the White-teethed Shrew in the British Isles,' *Proceedings of the Royal Society of Botany*, vol 164, p63 (1966)

DEWAR, S. *Witchcraft and the Evil Eye in Guernsey* (Guernsey, 1970)

DOBSON, R. *Birds of the Channel Islands* (London, 1952)

DRAPER, B. H. *Guide to Jersey and Guernsey* (Southampton, before 1879)

DUNCAN, J. *History of Guernsey* (London, 1841)

DURAND, R. *Guernsey Past and Present* (Guernsey, 1933)

——. *Guernsey under German Rule* (London, 1946)

DURY, G. *The Channel Islands*; in series Stamp, L. D. *The Land of Britain* (London, 1950)

ELHAI, H. *La Normandie Occidentale, Etude géomorphologique* (Bordeaux, 1963)

Elizabeth College Register 1898. History of the College, 1824–1873 (Guernsey, 1898)

GIRARD, P. J. *A History of the Bulb and Flower Industry in Guernsey* (Guernsey, n.d.)

——. *Early Crop Production in Guernsey* (Aberystwyth, 1966)

GRASEMANN and McLACHLAN. *English Channel Packet Boats* (London, 1939)

Guernsey Society, *The Guernsey Farmhouse* (London, 1963)

HARRIS, S. *Village Settlements in the Channel Islands* (Leeds, 1927)

HEAD, SIR G. *A Home Tour through Various Parts of the United Kingdom* (London, 1837)

HEYLIN, P. *A Survey of the Estates of France and of some of the Adjoyning Islands* (London, 1661)

HOOKE, W. D. *The Channel Islands* (London, 1953)

HUGO, V. *L'Archipel de la Manche* (Paris, 1883)

170

INGLIS, H. D. *The Channel Islands* (2nd edn) (London, 1835)

JEE, N. *Guernsey's Natural History* (Guernsey, 1967)

KENDRICK, T. D. *The Archaeology of the Channel Islands*, vol I (London, 1928)

LE HURAY, C. P. *The Bailiwick of Guernsey* (London, 1952)

LEMPRIÈRE, R. *Portrait of the Channel Islands* (London, 1970)

LE PATOUREL, J. (ed). *The Building of Castle Cornet* (Manchester, 1958)

LITTLE, B. *Saint Peter Port, its Story and its Buildings* (Guernsey, 1963)

McCULLOCH, E. (ed E. F. CAREY). *Guernsey Folk Lore* (London, 1903)

MACKENZIE, C. *My Life and Times. Octave 5 (1915–23) and Octave 6 (1924–32)* (London, 1966)

MARQUAND, E. D. *Flora of Guernsey and the Lesser Channel Islands* (London, 1901)

MARSHALL, M. *Herm, its Mysteries and its Charm* (Guernsey, 1958)

MAYNE, R. H. 'History of the Channel Island Mailships' *Guernsey Life*, vol 1, no 1 (December, 1966)

MOORE, R. D. *Methodism in the Channel Islands* (London, 1952)

MYHILL, H. *Introducing the Channel Islands* (London, 1964)

PHILLIPS, A. R. *Buses*, no 81 (December, 1961)

SKINNER, REV J. *Journal of a Tour to the Channel Islands* (MS, 1827)

TOMS, C. *The Ormer* (Guernsey, n.d.)

TUPPER, F. B. *History of Guernsey and its Bailiwick* (Guernsey, 1854)

VALLAUX, C. *L'Archipel de la Manche* (Paris, 1913)

WILLIAMS, T. E. *The Household Guide and Instructor, with Biographies of the Presidents of the United States of America and a Brief Outline of the History of Guernsey County, Ohio* (Cleveland, 1852)

WILSON, F. E. *Railways in Guernsey* (Guernsey, n.d.)

WOOD, A. and M. S. *Islands in Danger* (London, 1955)

WOOD, J. *Herm, our Island Home* (London, 1972)

INDEX

Figures in italic refer to plates

INDEX

174